Payback

By
S J Crabb

Also By S J Crabb

The Diary Of Madison Brown

Premier Deception

The One That Got Away
(Part 1 of The Hardcastle Saga)

A Matter Of Trust
(Part 2 of The Hardcastle Saga)

Coming soon

Falcondell
(The Devil's Son)

Operation Zodiac
(Bethany's Story)

Copyrighted Material

Copyright S J Crabb 2016
S J Crabb has asserted her rights under the Copyright, Designs and Patents Act 1988 to be identified as the Author of this work.

This book is a work of fiction and except in the case of historical fact, any resemblance to actual persons, living or dead, is purely coincidental.
This book contains Adult content and is not suitable for ages under 18.

Prologue

Vanessa closed the magazine that she had been reading. The advert had caught her attention and reminded her of some unfinished business.
She thought back two years ago. How different her life had been then. She was married to a self obsessed brute of a man who had been lined up as her husband for as long as she could remember. Her family had thought that it had been the perfect match. The marriage would unite the two dynasties and ensure its longevity. They hadn't realised what a truly abhorrent creature he really was. Surely if they had they would never have given the union their seal of approval. I say union rather than marriage because it was more like a dictatorship. Claude had been the most hideous, reprehensible, disgusting human being that Vanessa had ever had the misfortune to come across, and she had married him. It hadn't been that obvious at first, probably because he was on his best behaviour. However it soon became obvious that he had only married her for her inheritance and her bloodline. Being the daughter of a Lord and a well respected business man had many advantages to somebody keen to elevate himself up the social ladder. She in turn had been

dazzled by him. He had well and truly swept her off her feet.

The courtship hadn't been long. She fell for him hook, line and sinker and they were married shortly afterwards. The wedding had been the society event of the year if not the decade. The guest list was a veritable, Who's Who and it was a marriage made in heaven. If only she had known then what she grew to know, she would have realised that it was not Heaven but one made in Hell.

As time went on she began to realise the type of person that she had married. He soon started to bully her, both emotionally and physically. Any thoughts or suggestions that she had he shouted down. He belittled her opinions and made her out to be stupid and vacuous to his friends. In company he played the attentive husband but in private he ridiculed her and dented her confidence. He was always harsh in his criticism of her appearance and enjoyed comparing her unfavourably with their friend's wives. He called her dowdy and unattractive and declared her physically repulsive to him. Their sex life had never been good and he merely went through the motions to produce an heir. The fact that they hadn't managed it fuelled his anger and he blamed her for being barren. Vanessa however had thought it a blessing in disguise as the last thing she wanted was to bring a replica of him into the world.

Before long he started a series of affairs. He was very indiscreet about it and enjoyed taunting her with his exploits. He moved into his own room and even began to bring his conquests home. Soon she became a laughing stock. She lost her friends and her family blamed her for not being able to hold on to her man. Her own self confidence hit rock bottom. She even hated herself. They couldn't all be wrong. It must have been true what he said.

Soon she believed everything he told her and one day she decided to end it all. Unfortunately for her she was found before it was too late. She had taken a cocktail of drugs intending never to wake up. Her maid found her and raised the alarm.

She had then spent several months in an institution on suicide watch at the request of her "loving" husband. He had played a blinder. Everyone felt so much sympathy for him. He had tried to be a good husband but she had become unbalanced and needy. He told everyone that she had turned to drink, even though she never touched a drop. He lamented her downfall in public and celebrated it in private.

Despite her incarceration she was actually quite glad to be free from him. Life at the institution became her saviour. It was her sanctuary and she could finally live without the fear of him. He never visited, telling everyone that asked that he couldn't bear to see what she had become. It suited her well. He was the last person she wanted to see anyway.

Sadly her new found life was to be short lived. Her father died and she was his sole heir. She would inherit his fortune and title and so it was with a great deal of publicity that she was deemed cured of her depression and re united with her loving husband. He in turn would take her father's place as Chairman of the bank and she would resume her role as his loving wife. What she didn't realise at the time was that she had the power to divorce her despicable husband. Because she was in such a fragile mental state she just accepted everything that he told her.

Life carried on as before and she threw herself into social engagements and headed up various charities. Anything to escape from her loneliness and empty marriage. Claude was wrapped up with life at the bank and she was wheeled out only when he needed her beside him at the various functions and social engagements. Their marriage became one of convenience. They existed together as virtual strangers in private and a loving couple in public. However it soon became apparent that her husband was not as good a business man as her father had been. Stories began to reach her about his bad management and dodgy dealings.

He became increasingly difficult to live with and once again blamed her for his problems. Things were spiralling out of control until one day he appointed somebody new to the Bank. That man became his saviour and also much to her surprise hers. That man was Ben Hardcastle. He took over the everyday running of the bank, freeing Claude up from making any decisions of any importance. When they met at social functions she found herself drawn to him. He was extremely attractive and good company. They struck up an unlikely friendship and she began to very much look forward to seeing him again. She started to think of reasons to visit the bank and engineered many supposed chance meetings with him. Soon she became obsessed with him. He was everything her husband wasn't. Their relationship changed following an extremely dull charity event. Claude had reverted back to his philandering ways and was extremely indiscreet about it. At the dinner it was obvious that his latest conquest was also invited and he spent most of the evening with her. Vanessa was once again being publicly ridiculed and was the subject of a lot of gossip amongst the diners. Ben had noticed the situation and heard the rumours. He spent the evening keeping her company. That in itself wasn't surprising, after all she was his boss's wife and they were seated at the same table.

As the evening progressed they discovered that they had many things in common. She enjoyed his company and as it appeared, he enjoyed hers. When he asked her to dance she jumped at the chance, and when he took her in his arms she experienced feelings that she never had before. She longed for him to hold her close and his close proximity was sending alien feelings of longing and desire through her. Much to her surprise he appeared to feel the same. Claude had disappeared with his latest conquest which was no surprise to her. Noticing that she was alone Ben has whispered to her, inviting her to his room for a nightcap. She had not hesitated and had followed him to his room, after a discreet interval so as not to set tongues wagging. That night had been the best night of her life. Ben had taken her to places that she never knew existed. Never before had she experienced such feelings. Their lovemaking was intense and had carried on long into the night. She never wanted the evening to end and when it did she cried with the desolation that she felt on leaving him. Thus began a secret affair that re invented her. She felt desired and loved and truly blossomed as a person. She was in love and it was obvious for all to see. Even Claude began to notice that she had changed. She was more confident and had begun to take more care in her appearance. She went out a lot more and had developed a wicked sense of

humour. She had blossomed into a beautiful desirable woman and obviously no longer needed him.
Then it all changed. Claude saw her in a new light. He began to stay home a lot more. He demanded more of her time and started to make advances towards her sexually. They hadn't slept together for many years and the more she resisted him the more he tried.
Through all of this she was seeing Ben. They met as often as possible, which wasn't often enough as far as she was concerned. She could cope with her repulsive husband's advances as long as she had Ben in her life.
It wasn't long though before Claude grew impatient. The fact that she spurned him only made him want her more. One evening before she was due to meet Ben in secret, Claude struck. She was ready to go out and it soon became obvious that her husband had had too much to drink. He was waiting for her in the hallway. Blocking her exit he told her to stay with him that evening. They had a terrible argument and he struck her across the face. Pulling her into the drawing room he had then proceeded to physically assault her. She was no match for him and his attack lasted long into the night. There was nobody to save her as he had given the servants the night off. He raped her several times and beat her black and blue. By the time he had finished she was a quivering wreck and once again he had destroyed her.

The attack set her back years. Claude carried on as normal, offering her no apology, just telling her that she needed to be put in her place. She was his wife and her obligation was to him. She secreted herself in her room and didn't come out for days.

It must have been three days later that Ben came to the house. Claude had left and he came on the pretence of delivering some documents for Claude to sign. As soon as she saw him she broke down. He had been shocked and appalled and urged her to leave with him. She had been so tempted but during her time in her room she had had time to think. Despite her beating and mental torture she was no longer the woman she once was. Ben had shown her another way and a plan had begun to form in her mind.

As she remembered what happened next Vanessa smiled to herself. Ben Hardcastle had saved her not only once but twice. Without him she could never have carried out what happened next. Now as she looked at the advertisement she realised that she needed his help again. This time though he wouldn't know it but he would be saving himself too. It was time to get back in touch.

Chapter 1

Watching Ben bring the last of our suitcases inside my heart plummets. I feel so depressed at the thought that our idyllic holiday is now at an end and we are back to work on Monday. Ben looks over as he sets the last case down and smiles ruefully at me. "So here we are then," he says and moves towards me. Pulling me towards him he tilts my face towards his and staring gently into my eyes he plants a soft kiss on my lips. "Thank you for the best holiday that I have ever had," he says softly. This does nothing to raise my spirits, if anything it depresses me even more.

We have just spent two glorious weeks in the Maldives, with nothing but each other for company amid the Paradise Island that we called home for fourteen days and nights. There was no work, phones or computers, just us enjoying each other's company and relaxing from the stresses of the past few months.

As soon as I stepped through the door it all came flooding back and it is as if we never went away.

Ben laughs as he sees my face. I can't help but look upset. I had him all to myself for once and it is going to be hard to let him be once again absorbed into his demanding job. He is now the owner of eight

Department Stores, Kingham's included, where I work as the homewares buyer. They keep him extremely busy and he is always working, sometimes well into the night. Shaking me out of my depression he says, "Come on Bella, let's get a drink and leave the unpacking until tomorrow. We may as well make the most of our last night of freedom." Grinning at him I say, "What, you aren't even going to check your phone or e mails, you must be itching to take a sneaky peek?" Laughing he grabs hold of me and throws me over his shoulder. "You think you know me so well don't you? Well I still have a few surprises up my sleeve and the last thing I want is to start working as soon as I step foot inside the house. You are a much more attractive proposition." He carries me squealing into the kitchen and throws me unceremoniously down onto the settee. "Now stay there and I'll grab the wine. I have a feeling that this is going to be a long night."

A feeling of excitement grows within me at the thought of what he has in store. I will never tire of him. You would think that after two weeks together we would relish some time apart, this is so not the case. If anything the more I have of him the more I want. I have never met anyone who excites me as much as he does. I watch as he grabs a bottle of wine and two glasses. Looking suggestively towards me he says, "Come on then. You and I have to make the most of the last evening of our holiday, and I suggest we spend it in bed." I feel myself getting heated as he looks at me with a smouldering look and hate myself for my reaction as he laughs gently on seeing my flushed face. He always has this effect on me, even now after having been together for almost a year. I reach out and he pulls me up. This is one evening I am going to enjoy.

Chapter 2

The morning sun filters through a crack in the curtains and wakes me. At first I think that I am still in my hotel room in the Maldives and then with a sinking feeling I realise that I am back home. Turning over I am not surprised to see the empty space beside me. Despite a full on evening I knew that Ben wouldn't be able to resist the pull of his laptop for long and I know exactly where to find him.

Stretching out I savour the last few minutes of relaxation before I swing my legs out of the bed and search for my robe.

As I run the shower I think back to the events before our holiday. I wonder what life is like now for Nathan and Bradley in prison and shudder as I think of what might have happened. If Nathan had succeeded in framing me for his crime it would be me residing in a prison cell instead of him. It still angers me that he used me to try and steal millions of pounds from companies and individuals. His plan was to escape to another country and leave me to face the consequences. Thank goodness that Ben found me and saved me from him.

Stepping underneath the hot steamy shower I wonder

what the next few months will bring. Ben is adamant that he is giving up his job with the government organisation that he works for, flushing out criminals and bringing them to justice. I am not so sure. It was obvious when his Boss came to tell us what happened to Nathan that she wasn't going to let him go easily. It worries me as to what the future now holds. The thought of Ben having to go undercover worries me, not just because of the dangers that it involves but also what he may have to do in the line of duty. When I think of what Melissa and Tina, his two colleagues put themselves through it makes me wonder if Ben has also had to do similar things in the line of duty.

Pushing these thoughts firmly out of my mind I set off in search of him.

As I thought he is safely ensconced in his study, his laptop open in front of him. For a moment he appears not to notice that I have come into the room and I see that his expression is grim. As I approach the desk he looks up and for a moment he looks worried and then he closes the lid of the computer smiling gently. "Morning Bella, sorry about this, I woke up early and decided to make a start." Raising my eyes up I laugh. "It's no big surprise to me Ben; I am more surprised that it took you so long." Walking over to him I kiss him gently on the lips. In a flash he pulls me on to his lap and kisses me passionately. He runs his fingers through my hair and holds me tightly to him. "I love you Bella, more than you will ever know," he says squeezing me tightly. "Hey, what's all this about? You seem worried Ben." Wearily he looks at me and says, "Don't worry about it. I am paying the price for having two weeks off. It is going to take some time for me to deal with these e mails." Stroking my hair he says, "Come on lets have our breakfast. I'll tackle it after we've eaten."

We set about making our breakfast together and it is these times that I love the most. Just us in our own little world with everything and everyone shut outside.

After breakfast turning to Ben I say, "Listen, you get cracking on your e mails and I'll get ready and go to my parent's house and leave you in peace. I need to catch up with them and then I'll pick us up some food for later on the way home." Smiling at me Ben says, "Do you mind Bella? It would be a help to get started, but don't worry about the food, I'll take you out to eat instead."

Kissing him gently I say, "Ok, it's a date. But be warned, there will be no working this evening." Laughing he heads off back to his study and as I watch him go I can't help but feel a sense of gloom descend upon me, for some reason I feel unsettled and I just hope that I am wrong.

Chapter 3

"Bella, thank goodness you're back." Mum envelops me in a great big hug and as I hug her back I feel glad to see her. "Come on in and tell us all about your holiday, you lucky thing. Oh is Ben with you?" Mum says, looking around for him. Shaking my head I say, "No, he sends his apologies but he has had to stay behind to catch up with work." Mum raises her eyes up; she also knows by now what he's like so it comes as no surprise.
As we make our way to the kitchen I take in the familiar surroundings. I love coming home. Everything here reminds me of happy times spent with my family. I quickly shrug off the ones that I have with Nathan here. My parents adored him and were devastated when they found out what a criminal he turned out to be. As if she has a sixth sense my mother says in a low voice, "I had coffee with Marie yesterday, she is in a bad way." Startled I look at her. Marie is Nathan's mother and now a family friend. Our families grew quite close when Nathan and I were dating and despite everything we still love his parents. "Why, has anything happened to Nathan?" Despite everything I still care what happens to him. Mum shakes her head and with a worried

expression says, "He's having a terrible time in prison. Apparently he can't accept what has happened and is really angry. He takes it out on Marie and Tony and it is getting to the stage where they dread visiting him." As I listen to her I feel angry at Nathan. Sharply I reply, "Well he only has himself to blame. His actions have caused him to be where he is and it's wrong of him to take it out on them." Mum nods in agreement. "Apparently he is desperate for news about Melissa. She is all he can think of and wants his parents to track her down. He thinks she may be in Italy because it appears that she has a house there."

I don't say anything but I know that she is definitely not there. In fact who knows where she is but all I know is that she is probably on another job already. Melissa works with Ben and was sent to get close to Nathan and foil his attempt to defraud millions of people. He of course knows none of this and still thinks that they are in love and that she is probably in hiding somewhere. Once again I am reminded of the lengths that Ben and his colleagues go to in order to complete a mission. I am just glad that Ben has told them that he no longer wants to be a part of it. I don't think that I could bear the thought of him cosying up to another woman in the line of duty. Sipping tea with my mother the conversation turns back to my holiday and I spend a happy hour telling her all about it. I show her the photos that I took on my phone and once again feel depressed that we have left such a paradise behind. Mum interrupts my thoughts and says, "So are you back to work tomorrow?" Nodding I say, "Unfortunately yes. I am sure I will soon get back into the swing of it, I am just hoping for a quiet easy life from now on." Reaching over my mother squeezes my hand. "When I think of what might have happened I.." she sniffs and I smile reassuringly at her. Luckily for me Tina engineered my escape from Nathan which probably saved my life. To this day I still don't know what he had in mind for me back at the lodge but I know that it wasn't going to be pleasant. Tina, another of Ben's colleagues was posing as Bradley's girlfriend, Nathan's accomplice and without her help I may not be here now. Smiling reassuringly at my mother I say, "I know. Let's not dwell on what may have been. We will put it all behind us and move on." Jumping up my mother says, "Yes, thank goodness that it all turned out right in the end. Anyway let me cut you a slice of your favourite cake and I will fill you in on what's been happening in Emmerdale since you were away." Laughing to myself I am glad that I have my mum to bring me back down to earth.

On the drive home I think about Melissa. I was so

jealous of her when I thought that she was Ben's girlfriend. She has it all. Looks, personality and a wicked sense of humour. She is also the perfect actress and I can see why she is as successful as she is at her job. Men don't really stand a chance around her. Tina was different though. More ordinary and down to earth. I had counted her as a friend and I wonder where she is now. I try to turn my thoughts away from what happened. I need to re group and look to the future not the past. This was the main reason for our holiday. We decided to get away from the drama and focus on something good for a change.

Finding a new resolve I decide to try and forget about it all and look to the future instead. I feel excited at the thought of Ben and I making our life together. Finally we can be like every other couple and just live an ordinary life.

Chapter 4

When I get home Ben is still in his study. Laughing to myself I am aware that he probably hasn't moved since I left him so I decide to make him a drink.
He looks up as I enter the room and smiles softly at me. "How are your parents?" he says as I hand the drink to him. "Oh fine, although they did have some news about Nathan." He looks at me steadily and I tell him what my mother said. Looking thoughtful he says, "It will probably take him some time to adjust to it all. Maybe once the trial is out of the way he will come to terms with his situation." I look at him in alarm. "Do you think that I will have to testify?" Shaking his head he says, "Only if he pleads -Not Guilty. It's highly unlikely though given the amount of evidence against him. Either way he will have many years to come to terms with his new life."
I slump down into a nearby chair. "I just want to forget about it all now. I am back to work tomorrow and just want to get stuck in and forget about it all."
Ben gets up and comes and pulls me up. Taking my hands in his he looks lovingly at me. "I love you Bella. Whatever may happen next nothing will ever change

that. We have so much to look forward to and when this is all over we won't give it another thought." Nodding in agreement I reach up and kiss him lightly on the lips. "I love you too Ben. Despite what happened I am glad it did because it brought us together. How can I wish that never happened?"
We stand there just hugging until we are interrupted by Ben's mobile ringing. Sighing he moves away and answers it brusquely. He doesn't appear pleased to hear whatever the person is saying on the other end and just gives short non committal responses. Once again I feel uneasy and watch him trying to gauge what it's about. Hanging up he says, "Come on; let's go out for something to eat. This lot can wait." As I follow him I ask, "What was that all about, you seem tense?" Shrugging his shoulders he replies, "Nothing important. It can wait until tomorrow. I suppose like you I am just finding it hard to get back into the swing of things."
I follow him in silence and can't shake off the feeling that there was more to that call than he is letting on.

We drive to the local pub for dinner. I always love coming here. It is cosy and warm and the people in it are friendly. Over dinner we chat about our holiday and try not to talk about the past or work related subjects.
Just as we finish our meal his phone rings again. As Ben

looks at the display I notice a flash of irritation pass over his face and he rejects the call. "Who was that?" I say and he smiles saying, "Nobody important. They can wait until tomorrow. The only thing I want to do now is to take you home and do unspeakable things all night." He laughs as he sees my expression. It's either the wine, the heat from the open fire or the promise of what's to come that is the cause of the flush on my cheeks.

We spend a very intimate evening which rounds our holiday off nicely. When the alarm goes off at 6am we both groan. No more lie ins and just the promise of work to look forward to.

As we say our goodbyes Ben says, "Listen Bella. I will probably be really late home tonight. As well as sorting out everything that has piled up since our holiday I also have some unfinished business to take care of. It might be better if you can catch up with Phoebe and Boris, otherwise you'll be here alone." Sighing I say, "Listen don't worry. I will sort myself out. If they are unavailable I will just grab a meal for one and an early night. I'm not bothered so don't worry." Drawing me towards him Ben holds me tightly. "I hate this; I don't want to leave you even for a minute. I wish that you would reconsider moving to Head Office. At least then you would be near me." I push him away playfully. "You want everything your own way don't you? Well hard luck. I'm not going to make it that easy for you." He laughs but I sense that he is troubled about something. Hopefully he will sort it out today and then we can carry on as before.

We go our separate ways and my thoughts turn to the day ahead.

Despite my mood I am actually really pleased to get back to work. I am glad to see April my assistant buyer and she fills me in on what has been happening since I have been gone. Once she has told me what I need to know she says, "Oh I almost forgot to tell you. Simon is leaving." I look at her in amazement. Simon is the store manager. He was drafted in when Bob the previous Chairman sold out to Ben. He is very popular with the staff and I am surprised that he is leaving. "Since when, Ben didn't mention it?" April shrugs and says, "Maybe he doesn't know yet. It was very sudden. Last week he just came in one day and said that his wife had been offered a promotion at the bank that she works at and they would be re locating to Newcastle. He had secured a job up there and would be leaving in a month's time." As I take it all in I wonder if that was the call that had come through yesterday. I wouldn't have thought that it would have annoyed him to the extent that something obviously had, but then again I suppose it is inconvenient. Simon is a good manager. He is well respected and liked amongst the staff and certainly ran a happy ship.

Putting the information to the back of my mind I just get stuck into my work.

The time soon flies and I don't even stop for lunch. I don't hear anything from Ben and by the end of the day I am exhausted. The thought of an early night is an attractive one so I decide to just head off home and leave catching up with my friends for another night.

Chapter 5

During the next few days I hardly see Ben at all. I don't even have a chance to talk about Simon leaving and I can't wait for the weekend as we are meeting up with our friends Phoebe and Boris.
Friday night comes and when I get home I kick off my shoes with relief. Pouring myself a large glass of wine I flick through the answer phone messages. There is nothing there of interest so I decide to take my wine upstairs and promise myself a deep scented bubble bath. As I lie back in the hot sweet smelling water I feel it soak away the stress. Lying there I enjoy the feeling of relaxation that it gives me and watch the many candles that I have lit flickering in the dusky light.
I don't even hear the front door and am startled when Ben pushes the bathroom door open. As I look at him standing there my heart swells with love for him. He looks tired and weary, but still incredibly sexy. He still has his suntan and there is a hint of dark stubble on his face. His eyes darken as he sees me lying there and I smile sexily up at him and say, "What are you waiting for, aren't you going to join me?" He smiles wickedly and proceeds to take his shirt and tie off, not breaking eye contact with me for a second. Once he has discarded

his clothes I look at him standing there all bronzed and toned and my heart flutters in anticipation. Lowering himself into the bath he pulls me towards him. Tilting my lips up to meet his he kisses me so passionately that my insides melt with desire. He pulls me on to his lap and holds me firmly against him. I can feel his body responding to mine and enjoy the feeling of him so close to me. Trailing his fingers down the side of my face he then lowers them until he pulls me closer until he is inside me. The feel of him inside my body makes me complete. We move together kissing and touching each other until we both can stand it no more. The waves of release crash over us leaving us feeling totally relaxed and exhausted at the same time. Reaching over me he grabs the glass of wine and takes a large sip. Bringing his lips to mine he kisses me and I feel the warm fiery liquid entering my mouth. It feels so intimate and the pleasure it gives me excites me again. Dipping his finger in the glass he trails the liquid down towards my breasts and then licks it off following the trail. Then he takes my hand and leads me from the bathroom into the bedroom. Pushing me down on to the bed he kisses me all over until I can bear it no more. The need for him again is overwhelming and I pull him against me. As we make love once again I can't quite believe that he excites me as much as he does. There is nowhere that I would rather be than when I feel him inside me. As my orgasm explodes around me any worries or fears that I have go with it.

As we lie entwined together after our lovemaking I feel him stroking my neck and placing soft kisses on my back. I snuggle further into him enjoying the feeling of security that he gives me. Shattering the silence I say, "Is everything ok at work now Ben. Can you relax this weekend and leave it all until Monday?" Instantly I regret mentioning it because I feel him tense up beside me. In a low voice he says, "I can't promise the whole weekend but I am all yours tonight and then we will see for how long I can escape it all." Turning to face him I run my fingers gently down his face, stroking it as if to ease his troubles away. Catching hold of my fingers he kisses each one and then holds them to his cheek. "I love you Ben." I say softly. I say it to him all the time because I don't want him to ever forget it. He smiles and then says cheerily, "Come on, all of that exercise has made me hungry. Let's grab some food and bring it back to bed. I think we'll leave the plates behind though as I have a better idea of what I want to eat off of. Feeling myself blush again I am once again furious with myself for reacting to his obvious desire to embarrass me. I follow him as he laughs at my obvious discomfort.

We spend the rest of the evening in bed. Feeding each

other mouthfuls of finger food and then when it all gets too much again making love well into the night. Thank goodness it is the weekend. I am not sure that I could cope with a day at work after the night we've had.
It is extremely late into the night that we finally drift off to sleep.

Chapter 6

The next morning over breakfast I bring up the subject of Simon's resignation. "Did you know that Simon is leaving?" I ask Ben as I pour him some orange juice. He nods and says, "Yes Pete told me when I got back. Apparently he handed in his resignation when we were away. They have already advertised the position and will be interviewing next week." Looking at him in surprise I reply, "Golly, that's quick. When is he leaving?"
"Next month, but the sooner we find a replacement the better, then they can benefit from a hand over period." As we eat I mull it all over. It seems strange that it is all happening so fast. Watching me Ben says, "What are you thinking?" Shaking my head I say, "It just seems to be happening so quickly. I would have thought that he would give more notice than this, that's all. I will miss him though. He's a nice chap and was easy to get along with."
Ben nods in agreement. "Yes it was a bit of a surprise, but from what I understand his wife's promotion depended on her ability to move immediately. She has already gone so he is keen to follow her."
"Changing the subject are you still ok to meet up with

Phoebe and Boris this evening?" I say looking hopefully at Ben. He smiles and says, "Of course, I am looking forward to seeing them. Where are we going again?" "To that new restaurant in Town. I think it's Thai or Chinese, I can't really remember." The thought of meeting up with my best friend and her mad husband brightens my day. I love spending time with them and can't wait to tell them about our holiday. Ben laughs and says, "Judging by your expression you're looking forward to it. What are your plans for this morning?" Looking at him I say, "I haven't got any really. I might just potter around here. There are some jobs that need doing and I don't feel much like going out." Seeing his hopeful expression I put him out of his misery. "You can catch up with some more work if you want. That way we could go out tomorrow without it hanging over you. Leave all this and I'll tidy up." Ben smiles gratefully and kisses me before heading off to his study.

As I clear away I wonder who the new Store Manager will be. I hope that it is someone as nice as Simon. He will certainly be a hard act to follow.

The day passes by quite quickly and we are soon dressed and ready to meet Phoebe and Boris. On the way to the restaurant I say, "Did you get much done today Ben. I mean can the rest wait now until Monday?"

Reaching over Ben squeezes my leg. "I'm sorry Bella. I

know I ask a lot of you. Yes the rest can wait. Let's just enjoy the weekend."
As I settle back into my seat I feel happier. Hopefully the feeling of doom and gloom that has occupied me since our holiday was just the holiday blues.

Phoebe runs squealing towards me as she sees us coming. "Bella, I've missed you so much." She envelops me in a big hug and then does the same to Ben. Boris stands awkwardly on the sidelines laughing at his mad wife.
He shakes hands with Ben and then says, "Come on, Phoebe can't stand the cold for long, I had better get her inside in the warm." Laughing we follow them inside and are shown to a lovely table for four by the window. Phoebe and I chat incessantly about the holiday and what is going on in our lives. We don't come up for air and Ben and Boris just chat amongst themselves for most of the evening. The food is gorgeous and I am soon feeling rather full. Over coffee Boris turns to Ben and says, "I have heard that your old Bank is going through a rough period at the moment." Instantly I see Ben tense up and I look at him in surprise. Before Ben bought all the stores he worked as a trouble shooter for the bank before the banking crisis. He doesn't speak much about his time there but I know that he didn't enjoy it and it took its toll

on him. He looks at Boris with a sombre expression. "I know I have heard the rumours. Hopefully that is all they are." With interest I say, "What rumours are they?" Ben waves his hands dismissively and says, "Oh nothing much. It appears that they have made a few bad investments lately which are probably due to the people running it. The share price has plummeted and they are currently under investigation."

Boris looks equally sombre and says, "Because of all the trouble that the banks caused before the crisis any little thing affects the markets considerably. I have heard that they are moving in to assess the damage and try to limit the effects." Boris also works for a large bank in the city so I say, "What about your Bank Boris, will that be affected?" Shaking his head Boris replies, "I don't think so. There is nothing to signify that anything untoward has happened at my Bank but it makes everyone nervous when they hear of problems elsewhere."

Phoebe chips in and says, "Enough of all this. I for one don't want to hear about boring Bank business. When are we going out for a girly day again Bella?" Laughing we leave off the subject and return to more frivolous ones.

At the end of the evening Phoebe and I have made plans to meet up for a shopping day and we go our separate ways. I notice that Ben is quiet on the drive back and can't help but think that it has something to do with what we spoke about at dinner regarding the Bank. I noticed that his mood changed after that conversation and once again a feeling of doom and gloom comes over me. We don't speak about it again and in the end we have a nice relaxing weekend, pushing work very much to the background.

Chapter 7

Once again life takes on a regular pattern. I hardly see Ben due to his workload and when he comes home in the evenings he is shattered. I am also fairly busy at work which I don't mind as I love my job and enjoy the day to day life at the store.

It must be a couple of weeks later when Ben drops his bombshell. Coming home one evening I notice that he looks more strained than usual. Usually he comes straight over and gives me a kiss, but tonight he comes in and looks at me with an expression of such despair that my breath catches in my throat. "What is it Ben?" I say shakily, now extremely worried. He says nothing and just covers the distance between us and pulls me against him tightly. It is as if he is holding on to me as if his life depended on it and I am now extremely worried. Squeezing me tightly he buries his face into my hair and I can feel how tense he is. Pushing him away I reach up and touch his face, staring into his eyes. "Tell me, something's wrong, what is it?" Sighing he pulls me down next to him on to the settee and holding me against him he says, "I'm sorry Bella. I am afraid that something's come up that I have to deal with. It's nothing to do with the stores, just something that I worked on before I met you. It means that I may have to go away for a few weeks." Instantly alarm bells ring in my head. I know that he was working at the Bank that Boris spoke about at dinner before he met me and I also know that it wasn't a pleasant experience for him. Looking at him with what must be a confused expression I say, "But why do you have to go away, is it abroad?" Shaking his head he says, "No, but I can't rule out the possibility that I may need to travel. Despite the fact that I told my Boss I didn't want anything more to do with the organisation, it is unfortunately not that straightforward. This is something that concerns the job before I met you and I am afraid that only I can resolve it. The trouble is when I am on an operation I can have no contact with anyone outside of it. Therefore I have to stay at a different address until it is resolved." I can feel the tears welling up in my eyes but I blink them away. I must be strong for Ben. It appears that he has enough on his plate without me adding to his problems. Turning towards him I say, "But what about the stores. Who will manage them whilst you are away?"

"Oh they will be fine. Pete will take over for me and the store managers will continue to manage each individual store. Pete will be the only one who can get a message to me so if things go badly wrong I will be able to sort it out." Suddenly I feel worried. "What do you mean that

Pete will be your only contact? Can't I even call you?" Ben pulls me towards him and says gently, "I'm sorry Bella, no you cannot. It's like I said, I can't have any contact with anyone. It's why we don't usually have relationships. They get in the way of our jobs."
Angrily I move away, standing up and putting some distance between us. "But it's ok for Pete to call you. How will I even know if you're ok?" Sighing heavily Ben says, "I'm sorry Bella. I know that this is difficult. It is for me too. The last thing I want is to be dragged back into that world but I have no choice. It was never going to be easy getting away from it, but I can assure you I will try to resolve it as quickly as possible. If you need me for anything go and talk to Pete. He is the only one that knows my situation. He will help you."
I can't help it and the tears now fall freely. "I don't want to talk to Pete; I want to talk to you. It's not too much to ask is it?" I run out of the room sobbing and race up to the bedroom. Throwing myself on to the bed I don't care that I am acting like a child. It's not fair. I don't want Ben back in that world. Who knows what he will have to do and if it involves another woman then I don't think that I could bear it.
I feel him gently lifting me up from the bed and he holds me gently to him. "Please don't cry Bella. I love you so much and this is just as painful for me. I cling on to him

tightly still sobbing as he strokes my hair. He holds out a tissue to me and I use it to dry my eyes. I feel ashamed of my outburst and try to gather myself together. Sniffing I say, "When do you have to go?" There is a brief silence and then he says softly, "Tomorrow morning." I look at him in astonishment. I notice that he looks tired and strained and once again I feel bad. Mustering up what dignity I have left I smile weakly and say, "Then we must make the most of our last evening together." My words just seem to pain him more and he says softly, "I will do everything in my power to resolve this and get back to you as quickly as possible. There will not be a minute that goes by that I will not be missing you and just remember that I love you and just have faith in me that I will do nothing to hurt you, whatever you might hear."

Rather than reassure me his words only alarm me more. However I don't want to waste the small amount of time that we have left going over it all. Reaching over I kiss him gently on the lips. "I trust you Ben, I always have. Do what you have to do, but do it quickly. I will be here when you get back and don't worry about anything here whilst you are away." Looking at me his eyes darken and he says, "I don't know what I have ever done to deserve you Bella. I will never do anything that will ruin what we have." Then he kisses me passionately and for a while everything is forgotten whilst we make the most of our last evening.

Chapter 8

When I wake up the next morning Ben is gone. As I notice the empty space beside me I jump out of bed with a cry. Racing through the house I realise that he has left already and sinking down on to the stairs I cry uncontrollably at the thought that I never even said goodbye. After a while I pull myself together and even manage to laugh at how absurd I am behaving. Anyone would think that he has left me for good the way I am behaving. I must get a grip and just use the time to work hard and catch up with friends and family.
As I go into the kitchen to make myself a cup of tea I see a note from Ben.

Bella
I am sorry to leave before you got up but I couldn't bear to see you as I walked out of the door. Remember any problems talk to Pete. Stay strong and I will do my best to be back as soon as I can. Remember that I love you more than anything in the world.
Ben xx

His words make me cry again and once again the unwelcome thoughts of what he may have to do enter my mind. With a deep breath I set about getting ready. I admonish myself for how selfish I am. It is going to be harder for him and all I can think of is myself and my jealous thoughts. With determination I vow to stay strong and carry on as normal and then he will be back and all of this will be in the past.

I head off into work with a heavy heart. On seeing my expression when I enter my office my assistant April raises her eyes up. "You look awful Bella. Are you feeling ill?"
Laughing at her I say shakily, "Oh no I'm fine don't worry. Just a bad night that's all." Looking unconvinced she returns to her computer.
As I study my e mails I am surprised to see one from Simon the store manager. There will be a management meeting later on to introduce his successor. Goodness what with everything last night I completely forgot to ask Ben about Simon's replacement. They certainly didn't hang around and I feel curious as to who it will be. Turning to April I say, "Do you know anything about the new store manager April. There is a meeting later on to meet him." Swinging around to face me on her chair her eyes look bright with excitement. "Really, today. Oh my God I hope it's the guy I saw him with on my way in this morning. He is a total sex God." Laughing at her

obvious pleasure I say, "Well let's hope so for your sake then."

Thinking about it I feel quite excited to meet him. I hope that he is as easy going as Simon. I don't think that I can cope with much more at the moment.

After lunch I make my way up to Simon's office with the rest of the management team. I walk with Karen, my friend who buys for the fashion department. She too is excited and says, "Have you heard Bella, this guy is supposed to be gorgeous. If he is it will certainly brighten up the usually mundane management meetings." Laughing at her I say, "Yes April was equally pleased. I shall look forward to seeing what all the fuss is about."

As we enter the room and take our seats at the conference table I look with interest towards the new recruit. He is standing chatting to Simon near the window and I take the opportunity to study him. He is certainly drop dead gorgeous and actually looks like he has stepped out of one of the posters in menswear. He must be over 6ft tall with broad shoulders and despite his suit you can see that he has an incredible physique. His hair is dark and cut quite short and he has chiselled features that are set in concentration as he listens to Simon. Even from my seat I can see that he has incredible blue eyes and I notice with amusement that every woman in the room is openly staring at him in amazement. The men however look edgy and just a little put out. Moving my eyes away from him I take out my notebook and turn my phone off. Then Simon calls everyone to attention and addresses the room.

"Good afternoon everyone. I would like to introduce you all to Stephen De Souza, our new store manager." There is a general hum of noise as everyone says hi and I notice that he just nods generally and looks around the room with an air of indifference.

Simon carries on. "As you know I will soon be leaving and Stephen will be taking over the running of the store. There will be a short handover period and then he will be on his own. I hope that you will all give him as much support as you did me and I am sure that you will all enjoy working together." Then turning towards Stephen he says, "Over to you Stephen." Nodding towards Simon, Stephen stands up and faces the room. He speaks in a slow deep voice and says, "Thank you Simon. I will endeavour to carry on your good work at this store. You must all be wondering why I have been chosen to succeed Simon so let me fill you in. I have worked in stores since I left school. My jobs have taken me all over the world and I have worked myself up through the system in various positions. I have a broad understanding of how a store runs and have a wealth of experience to bring to the table. I will be working closely with you all to ensure the success of Kingham's for the future. I am a fair person but do not tolerate fools. I expect my management team to work hard and not become complacent. There is no room for error when I am in charge and I expect you all to give me 100% at all times. I will meet with you all individually over the next few days and discuss how we can move this store on to bigger and better things. For now though I am sure that you will join me in wishing Simon every success for the future and thank him for his sterling work here."

There is a general burst of applause and I notice that a few people around the table look a bit put out. I can understand why as Stephen was a little bit scary and brusque. I hope that it was just down to nerves. The last thing we all want is someone unapproachable and demanding.

As we file out of the room Karen nudges me and says, "What do you think about him?" Pulling a face I say, "I don't know yet. First impressions are saying he's quite intimidating." Karen laughs in agreement. "Yes, mine too. Sexy though." "And you a married woman, what would your husband say?" She grins and says, "I may be married but it doesn't stop me looking."

We go our separate ways and I laugh to myself. It is true

that he is good looking but there is more than that to a person and for some reason there is something unsettling about him. I am sure that it will all be fine but once again an uneasy feeling comes over me.

Chapter 9

The week drags on and I miss Ben for every second of it. True to his word I don't hear from him and it is almost unbearable. The house is empty and I don't look forward to going home every night on my own. Several times I think about contacting Pete to see if I can get a message to Ben but then my common sense takes over and I resist the urge.

Tonight I will be spared the empty house as we are all meeting after work for Simon's leaving drink at the pub near to the store. I walk over with April and Karen and am quite looking forward to an evening out. I could do with a good laugh as there hasn't been much humour in my life just lately.

When we arrive the pub is already packed and we join the queue at the bar. As I look around I can just make out Simon in the middle of a large group of people and nudge April and Karen. "Look there's Simon over there. Would one of you pop over and see if I can buy him a drink. I'll wait here to be served." Karen says, "I'll go, if you get served before I make it back can you order me a white wine?" I nod, "Of course, what about you April?" "Oh the same if you don't mind. Actually I just need to find the ladies, I won't be long." As they go their separate ways I look around me with interest. The whole store appears to be here, which doesn't surprise me as Simon is very popular. We will all miss him and for some reason I can't get as excited about his replacement as the others seem to be.

I feel as though I have been waiting for ages and don't appear to be getting any nearer to the bar. Karen pushes her way back and says, "Don't worry Simon says that he has already got several drinks lined up, but to thank you anyway." Laughing I reply, "Well maybe he could spare one of them each for us. We'll be lucky to get served tonight at all at this rate." April soon comes back and we stand about chatting whilst we wait.

It takes us about half an hour before we get the drinks and then we make our way to join the rest.

The volume is so loud and it is difficult to hear anything. I do manage to have a chat with some of my colleagues but its hard going. My feet are starting to ache and I would give anything to sit down.

As the evening wears on the crowd thins out and a table becomes available. We quickly grab it and Karen, April and I sink down gratefully onto the plush seats.

"Shall we order some food?" I say hopefully. I don't feel much like cooking when I get home and am starting to feel hungry. The others nod and once we have chosen I head off once again to the bar to place our order. As I wait patiently I am suddenly aware of somebody behind me standing very close. Looking around I am surprised to see Stephen, the new store manager waiting to order. I smile at him and he nods and then looks away. I turn back to the bar as the waitress asks me for my order and then make my escape once I have paid. When I join the others they want to know what happened. Karen says, "We noticed our new sex God behind you, did he say anything?" Shaking my head I say, "No, I smiled at him but he just nodded and looked away. He probably didn't know that I work at the store." April says, "I would queue for hours if he was standing next to me." We laugh at her wistful expression and I say, "What about Kevin I'm sure he would have something to say about your lustful thoughts towards another man." We laugh at her expression as she raises her eyes up dismissively at the mention of her boyfriend.

Simon soon comes to join us and we ask him all about his move and what his plans are for the future.

Before long Stephen comes up to speak to him and Simon introduces us all. He says, "Stephen allow me to introduce some of your buying team. This is Karen, the fashion buyer." He turns to Karen and holds out his hand to her. I watch in amusement as she turns pink as he takes her hand and she just mumbles a hello. April is similarly affected and then Simon says, "This is Bella our buyer for home wares." As I take his outstretched hand I see his eyes flash with what appears to be recognition. Then he says, "I'm pleased to meet you." Simon gestures for him to take a seat and he pushes in next to Karen. I laugh inwardly at her expression. She looks suddenly really tense and tongue tied and I enjoy seeing her discomfort. Stephen looks around and says, "Well ladies, it is great to meet you all. I am sure that we will all get to know each other over the coming weeks." I smile and as I catch his eye I feel as though he is scrutinising me. It unnerves me as I feel his piercing blue eyes staring at me. Turning to Simon to break away from his gaze I say, "Is this the last we will see of you. When do you actually leave?" Simon grins and says, "Yes lucky you. I leave tomorrow for pastures new. I may pop back from time to time but my new job starts on Monday so there is no rest for the wicked as they say."

We all laugh and then somebody else approaches Simon and excusing himself he walks away.

We all sit there awkwardly as Stephen looks around at us. I feel as though I should make conversation so say, "Do you live far Stephen?" He once again looks at me as though he is thinking of something else and then says, "Yes not far away. I have a flat on the other side of town. How about you Bella, where do you live?" I don't know why but I blush and say brightly, "Oh Just outside

Guildford." He pauses and then says, "It would be more convenient for you to work at Head Office, why don't you transfer there?" The others look embarrassed and I just say, "My job is at Kinghams. I love working there and have no desire to work at Head Office." He studies me intently and I feel unnerved. I wonder if he has heard about Ben and I's involvement and is curious. He then turns his attention to Karen and asks her about her home life. I catch April's eye and she grins at me. It is obvious that we all feel really on edge around him and I just hope that it's because we don't know much about him yet. After about ten minutes he gets up and excuses himself and we all breath a big sigh of relief.

"Well!" says Karen, exhaling sharply. "He certainly has an aura about him." She fans herself and we all burst out laughing. We must stay for about half an hour more and then all head off home. Once again I dread returning to the empty house, but as it's late at least I just need to get some sleep.

Chapter 10

I have decided that I will just throw myself into work whilst Ben is away. Even though it is the weekend I head off to work to catch up with a few things. When I arrive I bump into the homewares department manager. "Hi Christine. How are you?" I say, smiling at my friend. She pulls a face and looks very stressed. "Oh I'm fine but I am two staff down today and can only cover the department with a skeleton staff. I don't know how I will manage the breaks." Feeling sorry for her I say, "I'll cover the breaks don't worry. It will do me good to spend some time on the shop floor." Her face lightens up and she looks at me gratefully. "You are an angel Bella. You don't know what a hole you have dug me out of." Laughing I head off to my office.

True to my word I head off to cover the morning break. Because it's Saturday the store is busy and I really enjoy myself. It is a change from my usual routine and just what I need to forget about Ben for a while. I am almost sorry when I have to return to my office.

Lunch time comes around and I head back to the department. On my way I see Stephen in the distance. He is walking purposefully towards the lift and I see many eyes turn his way as he goes. He however appears oblivious to the attention and seems to have an air of arrogance about him. As I watch from afar I suddenly see one of the customers racing after him. She appears to be calling him but he ignores her. Watching with interest I see her catch him up and pull on his arm. She is smiling and looks as if she knows him. He spins around and I watch as her smile falters at whatever he is saying to her. She looks confused and he looks annoyed. Intrigued I wish that I could hear their conversation. Almost immediately he strides off, leaving a very confused customer behind him.

My curiosity getting the better of me I walk over to where the woman is standing. Approaching her I say, "Can I help you madam?" I notice that she is about my age with long dark hair. She is quite attractive and is wearing a large puffa jacket and jeans. Shaking her head she says, "Oh, no thank you." She is still looking incredulously in the direction that Stephen went so I say, "I saw you talking to Stephen, do you know him?" Looking at me with a confused expression she says, "Did you say Stephen?" I nod and she says, "That's probably why." Now it's my turn to look confused and I say, "Why what?" Taking a deep breath she says, "I thought he was someone else. He is the spitting image of the person I thought he was. In fact his perfect double. It was quite strange really. He obviously isn't because he looked right through me as if he didn't know me." Intrigued I ask, "Who did you think he was?" Laughing nervously she says, "Come to think of it he couldn't have been. The person that I thought he was wouldn't be in a store like this and certainly not dressed so well. It's incredible the likeness though." Feeling fascinated I probe further, "That's so strange. Who did you think he was?" She appears to be relaxing slightly now and laughs saying, "I thought that he was my boyfriend's brother Joey. They live not far from here but Joey hasn't been seen in ages. The last I heard of him he was working away. Nobody knows what he was doing but the rumours were that he had a rich girlfriend and was living with her." Smiling at her I say, "Your boyfriend will be surprised to hear that his brother has a double." Instantly her expression changes and her eyes cloud over. "He won't care. He is away at the moment and I haven't heard from him. They also don't get on so even if I did hear from him he wouldn't be interested." Shocked I watch as her face crumples and tears run down her face. I put a hand on her arm and say, "Are you ok?" Sniffing she says, "Sorry, you don't want to hear about my problems. It's just that I miss him so much and when I saw Joey, I mean Stephen it was like Mikey was here, they look alike you see." Impulsively I hug her and she looks surprised. Laughing at her expression I say, "I'm sorry. I am missing my boyfriend too. He is also away and I also miss him every single minute of the day. Her eyes look at me with compassion. "I'm sorry to hear that. I hope that he comes back soon." Just then her phone rings and she rummages in her bag to find it. Realising that I should be at my till I say, "Anyway I will leave you to it. It was good to meet you. Stay strong, hopefully he will be back soon." She smiles at me as she retrieves the phone from her bag. "Thank you for being so kind." She then answers the phone and moves away chatting to whoever called.

As I make my way over to the Pay Point I think about what has just happened. She seemed so convinced that Stephen was this man called Joey. It was obviously not given his reaction to her and I laugh at how foolish she must be feeling now.

The rest of the day passes quickly and I am almost sorry when it ends. I have had so much fun working on the shop floor. Even after my cover had finished I decided to stay and help. If nothing else it helps to hear the customer comments on the ranges and see for myself what they buy and what looks good in the displays. I have learned a lot and vow to spend more time with the customers in future.

On returning home that evening I realise how tired I am.

I physically ache and guiltily I remember that I haven't exercised in weeks. Perhaps I should go the gym after work. This would be the perfect time to get back into shape. It would also help kill time after work and give me something else to focus on. I hate being at home without Ben. Everything reminds me of him and how much I miss him. I decide that starting tomorrow I will go to the gym and try to channel my feelings into something positive.

Chapter 11

The next day is Sunday and I have a day off. I am looking forward to it as I have been invited to spend it with my friends Phoebe and Boris. They don't live far and I enjoy spending time with them. I told them that Ben was away working and thankfully they haven't questioned me much about it. I can't tell them the real reason for his absence as they don't know about his other job as it is a secret one.

It doesn't take me long to reach their house as they moved nearer to us a few months ago. I absolutely love spending time with my best friend and have been looking forward to seeing them both all week.

As soon as I park the car next to Phoebe's little Fiat she appears as if by magic outside. Flinging her arms around me as I exit the car she gives me a huge hug. "Bella, it's great to see you. Come on in, Boris is making us some tea and I can't wait to hear your news." Laughing I allow myself to get dragged along behind her and as I enter their beautiful home I immediately feel relaxed.

I used to live with Phoebe in a little flat in town. We loved living together and shared many happy memories together. We both met our partners and Phoebe and

Boris got married and moved to the neighbouring village. I do miss our life at the flat though. It was good to have someone to mess around with and share my innermost thoughts with.

Phoebe drags me into the kitchen and announces my arrival to Boris in her dramatic fashion. "Bo, Bella is here at last. Crack open the teabags and don't spare the sugar. We have a lot of catching up to do." Boris grins at me and winks and then looks fondly at his wife. "She's missed you Bella, I'm afraid you are not going to get off lightly today. In fact I'm quite relieved you are here. I may even get some time to do something other than the endless list of jobs that she usually gives me at the weekend." Phoebe pretends to look annoyed and wags her finger at him. "Don't give us the husband under the thumb routine. I'm lucky if you even start one of the jobs I give you before you're distracted by a television programme or article in the newspaper." Boris laughs and coming over lifts her high into the air and then kisses her as she wriggles to free herself."

Watching them I am reminded of Ben again and how much I miss him. It physically hurts that I can't see him and the fact that I can't even talk to him just adds to the torture.

Phoebe struggles to get away and says with mock anger, "Put me down Boris. See you're already trying to get out of making the tea." Laughing he releases her and returns to his task. Phoebe raises her eyes up and says, "Come on Bella, let's sit down and you can tell me what's going on with you."

We sit in the kitchen chatting about things in general and then I mention my new boss Stephen. Phoebe listens with interest as I describe him and then I tell her about the customer in the store. She looks interested and says, "Goodness, how intriguing. You know apparently everyone has a double out there somewhere. I would love to meet mine. I bet we would get along really well and have loads in common. We may even find that we were really twins that had been separated at birth and due to a cover up at the hospital one of us had really been sold to fund a new operating table." Boris snorts with laughter as he listens in whilst he fixes a shelf on the wall. "Only you would think like that P. I can't imagine that there is anyone else out there like you, in fact it doesn't bear thinking about." I laugh as Phoebe throws a cushion in his direction. He catches it and throws it back at her and then they dissolve into hysterical laughter.

I look at them both fondly. Theirs is such a happy house. I have never met two people who suit each other as well as they do. Life with Ben is much more intense. He is always so busy and when we do have some precious time together it is all we can do to keep our hands off each other. At first I thought it was just because our relationship was new, but it has been well over a year now and we are still insatiable. As I think about him my expression must have changed because I notice that Phoebe looks at me with concern. I then notice her give a worried look to Boris who suddenly looks uncomfortable. He gives her a slight shake of the head as if warning her against saying anything and I look at them both in surprise.

"What's the matter guys. Is there something wrong?" Looking worried Phoebe glances nervously towards Boris who looks suddenly very interested in his job. Sighing she turns to me and says, "I'm sorry Bella. We have been rattling on about anything and everything but there is one subject that we haven't touched on. What is happening with Ben at the moment?" Looking at her in surprise I just say lightly, "Oh nothing much. Ben is away at the moment for work and I am really missing him."

Looking uncomfortable she says, "Oh, where has he gone?" As I study her expression I get the feeling that they know something that I don't and I suddenly feel worried. "What is it Phoebe? I can tell that you want to tell me something, is it concerning Ben?" Phoebe blushes and looks towards Boris for support. Putting the

shelf down he comes over to join us looking awkward and sits down next to her. As they both sit there looking anxiously at me I have a feeling that I am not going to like what they are going to say.
"What is it, you're worrying me?" I say, my stomach churning at what it could be.
Sighing Phoebe says, "It's probably nothing and we were in two minds whether to say anything at all but I'm sorry I can't not tell you." I am now feeling extremely alarmed and say, "Just tell me Phoebe. I want to know, is it Ben?"
She nods awkwardly and says, "Boris told me a couple of days ago that there is a rumour going around at work that Ben is back at the bank and has been creating lots of unrest and worry. Apparently the last time he worked there lots of people lost their jobs and then the collapse of the banking industry happened. People are worried that something big is going on and it is making them uneasy."
Shaking my head I say, "I expect that he's been asked to sort something out that has occurred regarding the time that he was there. It is probably nothing and he is certainly not going to be there for long." Looking a little relieved Phoebe says, "Has he said anything to you about how long he is going to be there. Is he there today?" Squirming under their scrutiny I don't want to

tell them that I haven't even spoken to him for over a week now. I try to gloss over it and say, "Not really, but he is so busy he hasn't had the time to chat." Once again I notice a look pass between them and then to my surprise Phoebe comes over to me and takes my hand in hers. Looking at me with concern she says, "I'm sorry Bella but there is something else I must tell you. It's probably nothing and we will laugh about it but I need to let you know." Now I am extremely worried and say, "What is it?" Boris looks down at the floor in embarrassment and Phoebe says gently, "There is also a rumour, and I must just stress that it is only that, that Ben is spending a lot of time with the owner of the bank Vanessa Montague." Surprised I laugh nervously saying, "What's the problem with that? He is doing a job for her so of course they will be spending time together." Blushing Phoebe says, "The rumours are that Ben and Vanessa were once extremely close. Many people think that he was having an affair with her when she was married and that he was somehow involved when her husband committed suicide." I can feel the blood pumping in my head as I dread hearing what I know she is about to say. "Word is that they are close again. They have been seen out on the town and appear very cosy together. One of Boris's colleagues said that he saw them both getting into a cab outside a hotel the morning

after a banking function. It appeared that they had spent the night there and seemed very close the next day."
As I take in her words and see their concerned faces I feel frozen to the spot. It is my worst nightmare to hear what she says but I can't let them know my fears. Ben is doing his job and for whatever reason it involves spending time with this woman. The thought of what he may be doing sends daggers through my heart but I must not crumble in front of my friends. Somehow I muster a nervous laugh and say, "I can see that it looks bad but I can assure you both that there is no mystery. I know all about it and Vanessa is just a good friend of Ben's. They stayed over because it was late and they had an early meeting. You know what Ben's like. He is such a flirt and they have a close friendship, nothing more." As I say the words I notice that Phoebe looks relieved and Boris smiles thinly. Needing to change the subject I brush it all off. "Anyway, when I see him later I'll tell him, it will amuse him to be the subject of so much scandal." They both laugh but I am not sure that I have convinced them of anything.
The rest of the day is spent talking about other things but my thoughts keep on turning back to what I have just heard. All I want to do is to go home and curl up in a miserable ball. The thought of Ben with another woman is devastating. I feel as though my heart has been frozen

and although outwardly I appear calm and relaxed, inside I am a mess. I know that Ben and his colleagues do more than I care to think of when they are undercover but I thought that that life was behind him now. I don't know how I am going to get through this.

Chapter 12

Once again I decide to throw myself into work. I have brought my gym bag with me as I have decided to start going to the gym after work to occupy my mind and vent some of the frustration that I am feeling.
Ever since Phoebe told me about Ben I can think of nothing else. I even considered phoning Pete and asking him to get Ben to call me. The sound of his voice would reassure me but I can't contact him just to alleviate my own fears and worries.
After turning on my computer I notice an email from Stephen summoning me to a meeting in his office at 10am. Mentioning it to April she suddenly looks worried. "I wonder what it's about?" She says, looking anxiously at me. Laughing it off I say, "It's probably nothing. Now that Simon has left he is getting down to the job in hand. I should think it's about his plans going forward." April pulls a face and says, "That's what I'm worried about."
Smiling to myself I am amused by her reaction. April always thinks the worst and expects doom and gloom around every corner.
After sorting out some orders it is soon time for my

meeting. As I approach Stephen's study I am surprised to see my friend Karen coming out and I notice with alarm the tears running down her face. Pulling her aside I say, "What's the matter Karen is everything alright?" She shrugs and says, "Oh Bella, it was awful. He was so cold and absolutely tore strips off me." Before she can elaborate the door to his office flies open and Stephen stands there looking annoyed. "I don't like to be kept waiting Miss Brown. Save your cosy chats for your own time not mine." He stands there holding the door open and Karen scurries away. My knees shaking I walk past him into the office. It is like I have been summoned to the Headmasters office and I feel as though I am not going to like what I am about to hear.

Gesturing for me to sit down Stephen closes the door behind him and then sits down at his desk opposite me. He suddenly looks me directly in the eye and with a serious expression says, "I will not beat around the bush, the figures for your department are not looking good and I have some serious concerns." To say I am shocked is an understatement and for a minute I don't know what to say. He carries on without waiting for me to react. "I would have expected a much higher growth figure given the current climate and so it is obvious that we have some work to do." Leaning back in his chair he fixes me with his hard gaze and I hate myself for not finding any words with which to defend myself. He is looking at me pointedly and then says, "Well. Any ideas?"

I can feel my anger rising but I will not give him the pleasure of seeing me crumble like Karen obviously did. Clearing my throat I stare back at him and say, "What do you suggest then? I would welcome any help or suggestions that you may have as you are obviously basing your figures on some experience that you have of the current market." I can tell that he is annoyed by my response and he snaps. "It is not for you to question my analysis but to defend your performance. I would suggest that you return to your department and compile a report for me to be handed back to me by the end of the day. I want a list of your current suppliers and your trading terms. I also want a brief history of your dealings with them and why you think that they are the best supplier for us to deal with. Maybe then I can gain an understanding of our position and then we can assess how we will move forward."

Leaning towards me he looks at me with a stony face. "I expect my staff to give their job 100% and I don't tolerate complacency. It is my job to get the best from this store and currently it looks like I have a lot to do. This store could be more profitable and I am leaving no stone unturned. Can I count on you to back me up or should I reconsider your position within this store?"

I just stare back at him not knowing quite what to say. Gathering myself I just nod and say, "Of course you can. I will have the report ready for you by the end of the day." He looks at me for a second and then gives the briefest of smiles. "Ok then you may go." Standing up I go to leave, I cannot get out of here fast enough. As I get to the door he suddenly adds, "Miss Brown. Don't think that you will get preferential treatment because of who your boyfriend is. If anything I expect more of you." I freeze, my hand grasping the door handle. Suddenly I feel anger surging through me. I stop and look back at him. Walking carefully back over to his desk I fix him with an unwavering look. In a hard voice I say, "I can assure you that I expect no preferential treatment. If anything this store means more to me than any of you. If you think for one minute that I don't give this job my all then you are very much mistaken Mr De Souza. You will have your report as requested by the end of the day and I will welcome your feedback. Now if you will excuse me I have a lot to do and I am sure that you do too." Spinning on my heels I don't even give him the satisfaction of a response and I march out of the room hating him more than I have ever hated anyone before in my working life.

Chapter 13

April is horrified when I tell her of my meeting. "We're going to get fired," she cries in dismay. Shaking my head I try to sound reassuring and say, "Nobody is going to be fired. We will sort out this report for him and then do whatever he recommends. He is just throwing his weight around that's all. I am sure that he will calm down when he has settled in. He will soon see how hard we all work."

April still looks worried but I can't help that. She is a born worrier anyway and nothing I will say will stop that.

As the day goes on I start to feel angrier and angrier. Thoughts of what Phoebe and Boris told me merge with my anger towards Stephen. Despite having such a mammoth task to complete my thoughts cannot turn away from Ben and this other woman. Images of them together plague my mind and a huge ache has formed in my heart. The memories of Melissa and Tina and what they did to bring Nathan and Bradley to justice play on my mind and are replaced with images of Ben and this other woman.

When April goes to lunch I tell her that I will carry on with the report. She offers to forego her own lunch hour but I reassure her that I can cope. I appear to have lost my appetite anyway.

As soon as she leaves I am on the Internet looking for articles about Vanessa Montague. There are several as she is quite the socialite. Seeing her staring out at me from the screen a knife twists in my heart. She is a beautiful woman. She has long dark hair and a very slim figure. Her eyes are her best feature and are a smoky bluey grey that stare out at me with a vulnerability that is appealing.

Obviously she is immaculately dressed and is pictured with many a handsome man at various functions. Feeling sick I continue to delve into her life.

I see an article written about her and her husband Claude Montague. Looking at him I notice that he has a cruel looking face. He has his arm casually around her waist in the picture but she looks tense and tired. Despite being well turned out her eyes look dead in this photograph and she is staring unsmiling into the camera. His smile also appears false and I notice that he has a hard glint in his eyes. If pictures tell a thousand words then this one delivers magnificently. It is obvious that theirs is not a happy marriage. Fascinated I continue my investigations. There is an article about Vanessa that shocks me. It is reported that she has gone off the rails and has been admitted to a mental institution. The article is an interview with her husband who states that he will stand by his wife but he had to get her the help that she badly needs. He was worried that he would return home one day to find that she had taken her own life and he could not live without her.

There are many photographs of him and articles about his suspected affairs and gossip about their relationship. The hour soon flies by and as I hear April returning from lunch I guiltily flick off the Internet and try to make it look as though I have been working.

Once again we get stuck into the report but my head is buzzing with the information that I have seen. April looks at me with concern and says, "Is everything ok Bella. You seen distracted?" Shrugging I say, "Oh I'm fine. Maybe skipping lunch wasn't such a good idea. Perhaps I should stop for a bit and get a coffee to keep me going."

April nods saying, "Of course you should. You go and have a break and I'll carry on here. Take as long as you need I'm sure that this won't take much longer anyway." Gratefully I head off outside and take in a deep breath. I decide to grab a coffee from a nearby coffee shop and try to process the information that I have just seen.

The coffee shop is busy and I wait in the queue distracted by my thoughts. As soon as I get my coffee I tuck myself away in the corner. I can't help myself and pull out my I pad.

Once again I start looking for information about Vanessa. I come across an article about her father. Lord Montague was a respected Banker who had run the bank that his father had founded meticulously. With interest I read about him and his family. His wife was beautiful and I can see the similarity with Vanessa. They led a charmed life. There are no negative reports or bad press about them and they appear a happy family.

I follow their life with interest. There are articles about them at various functions, on holidays and many photos showing their many homes. Fascinated I continue to delve and have soon built up quite a picture of their lives. I am conscious of the time and decide to carry on later at home. However before I close the I pad one photograph leaps out at me shattering my heart in an instance.

Ben is staring out at me, smiling seductively at the camera standing next to a positively glowing Vanessa. Feeling sick I continue to read the caption. It says, prominent banker Ben Hardcastle with Vanessa Montague at a charity event. My eyes well up and through my tears I can tell that they are more than just friends. It is obvious from their body language and I can see it in their eyes. Her face looks animated and she is looking at him with such love and adoration. He looks relaxed and happy and his eyes are sparkling and their hands are brushing against each others.

Snapping the cover closed I close my eyes, trying to get the image out of my mind. Once again fear and anger rise up within me and abruptly I leave the coffee shop and head back to work with everything buzzing around in my mind.

I know in my heart that they were lovers. It was obvious from the picture. I am not sure when it was taken; I forgot to look and dread the thought that it is a recent one.

Reaching my office I try to focus on the job in hand. I am thankful that I have such a great assistant and April does much of the work for me. I am cross with myself for letting my curiosity get the better of me but more than that I am cross with Ben. How could he just take off and leave me? Surely I deserve more than this. I know that he has this other life but he assured me that he was leaving it behind him when we got together. How could he go back to spending time with her whilst I am expected to wait for him at home, asking no questions and pretending that he is away on a business trip? It is obvious from Phoebe and Boris that he is not being discreet and that everyone assumes that he is back with Vanessa.

Interrupting my thoughts April says with satisfaction,

"There all done. Let's see him pull this to pieces."
Shaking myself out of my thoughts I smile at her and say, "Thanks April. I couldn't have done it without you. Hopefully we have done what he wants and he will see that we have run everything as it should be." She nods but still looks worried. "I hope so. I am still worried though. By the sound of it he is a bit of a tyrant so I wouldn't put anything past him." I smile at her trying to put her mind at ease but I also share her worries. Stephen is a bit of an enigma to me. I am surprised that he was chosen for the job as he is poles apart from Simon his predecessor. Once again I feel annoyed at Ben. How could he leave us with a monster in charge and then cut off all communication?
April gathers her belongings together and says, "Would you like me to drop off the report on my way out?" I notice her reluctant expression and say, "Don't worry, you've done enough. I'll drop it in. Have a good evening, and thanks again, I really appreciate the effort you have put into it." Smiling at me April leaves, the relief evident on her face.
With a sigh I gather up the report and my gym bag. I am grateful that I have something to do after work as I know that I would just spend the evening torturing myself with more research into Ben and Vanessa.
I head off up to Stephen's office to deposit the report on

my way out.

Chapter 14

The gym is a hive of activity when I arrive. I haven't been for so long and feel guilty that I have neglected my fitness. As I change I feel relieved that I didn't bump into Stephen when I went to his office. I am not sure that I could have coped with another run in with him.
Once I am changed I run through a programme with the resident fitness instructor. I channel all of my negativity into the session and try to switch my mind off.
Once we have finished I decide to round off the hour with a go on the running machine. It must be my state of mind because I just feel the need to keep going. I don't care that I should take it easy on my first visit and plugging in my headphones I start running. However as much as I try the image of Ben and Vanessa won't leave me and so I turn the machine to go faster. The music is pounding in my ears and I just go faster. It is as though I am running away from everything. Images of Ben, Vanessa and Stephen race through my mind and I start to sprint to escape them, my tears blinding me.
I am not sure how long I run for. I don't even register where I am; just continue to run in my desperate need to escape. Suddenly I am conscious that the machine is

slowing down. In alarm I notice that someone is standing beside me and has turned the machine off. Before I can even register who it is I am plucked off of the machine in one fell swoop and pulled against a broad muscular chest. The music is still playing in my ears and I cannot hear or see who has interrupted me. I feel myself being lifted off my feet and carried from the Gym. Then I am deposited on to a seat in the corridor and I look up in bewilderment to see an extremely angry Stephen looking down at me. He is also in his Gym attire and despite my shock I can see that he obviously spends a lot of time here due to his immense physique. His eyes flashing I can see him saying something but I can't hear what. Then I realise that I still have my headphones in and wearily I turn off the music and take them out. Gathering myself together I notice with a sinking feeling that I am drenched with sweat. My legs are shaking and I feel weak and dizzy. Sinking back against the chair I feel a bottle of water placed in my hand as Stephen says tersely, "Here drink this. Slowly though and drink it all." Gratefully I drink the water, the realisation sinking in that I have totally overdone it. When I have finished Stephen sinks down on to his knees in front of me and stares at me angrily. "What on earth are you playing at? You could have seriously injured yourself. Do you know nothing at all about fitness? You were lucky that I

noticed. Any longer and you would have collapsed and probably done yourself no end of damage."
Feeling like a complete fool everything suddenly explodes within me. Pushing him away I try to stand up, my legs shaking from the effort. "Thank you for your concern." I say with what I hope is a strong voice but in reality is more than a whisper. "I'll be fine now. I'll just shower and then go home. Sorry to be a burden to you."
Looking at me with exasperation Stephen grabs hold of my hand. "You are going nowhere until you have recovered. If you think that I am going to let you out of my sight until then you are mistaken. Come on, I'll get you another water and you can sit down for a bit until you are ready to change."
Shaking my head I protest but he is having none of it. He grabs another bottle of water and then pulls me down on to the seat beside him, effectively trapping me in the corner. His leg pushes against mine and I shrink away from him. Turning to look at me I notice with surprise that his expression softens.
"I'm sorry Bella. I feel responsible. Perhaps I put too much pressure on you today and it was too much. I forget that not everyone works like I do and I apologise."
This change of attitude surprises me and the fact that he is being so kind wrong foots me and tears spring to my eyes.

He looks at me with a worried expression and using his fingers wipes my tears away. I try to shrink away from him further into the corner but there is nowhere to go. I feel trapped and confused and just sit there next to him willing myself not to dissolve into a snivelling wreck. We don't speak and after about ten minutes he says, "You look a bit better now. Why don't you go and get a shower and then meet me back out here and I'll take you for something to eat. You can't drive in the state you are in and as I am famished you can keep me company." Looking at him in surprise I shake my head. "Oh it's fine. You've been very kind but I feel better now. I'll just go off home and get something there." His eyes flash and he says, "I'm not taking no for an answer Miss Brown. As I said, I will meet you out here and I will take you out for something to eat. I would never forgive myself if I let you drive home in the state you are in and something happened to you. I am sure that I would have a lot of explaining to do when Mr Hardcastle returns." At the mention of Ben my heart aches once again. Bitterly I say, "Oh I'm sure that he won't mind. He has other things occupying his thoughts at the moment anyway."

Instantly I regret my words as he looks at me in surprise. Blushing I try to stand up and luckily he lets me pass. As I brush past him he catches my arm and says in a softer voice, "Its ok, I promise not to grill you about work. It would be good to have some company for a change and you look like you could do with a distraction."

The fact that he is being so kind and the fact that my head is swimming with images of Ben and Vanessa I find myself agreeing to go to dinner with him.

As I get showered and dressed I think about the state that I got myself into. I am sure that I am being irrational but something is bugging me about the whole thing. It's been two weeks now and still no word from Ben. I know that he is not far away and I can't understand why he won't even call me. I know that I can't go on like this though. I need to speak to him and decide that I will speak to Pete first thing tomorrow morning.

When I get to the reception I can see Stephen waiting for me. He is dressed in jeans and a T shirt that accentuates his muscular body. He is quite a striking figure waiting there and I notice that he is the subject of much scrutiny from some of the other gym customers.

As he sees me he smiles briefly saying, "Ready?" Nodding I fall into step beside him and he says, "How are you feeling now. You had me worried there?"

Grimacing to myself at the knowledge that he found me in such a mess I smile weakly saying, "I'm fine thank you. I am sorry that you had me to deal with. I am sure that all you really wanted was to spend time at the gym after work and then get off home." Surprisingly he laughs, a sound that I do not associate with him and says, "All I do is work and go to the gym. It was a distraction from my normal routine and at least it means that I have company for dinner. Usually I have to make do with my own." I look at him in surprise. "Don't you have friends or family for company?" Turning to look at me he grins ruefully. "Well despite the fact that I am obviously great company and make friends easily, you may be surprised to learn that no I do not. My family live far from here and any girlfriends I have turn into jealous monsters that are more trouble than they are worth, so I prefer to just work instead."

Before I can reply he stops outside a Chinese restaurant. "Come on, this is a good place to eat. I hope that you like Chinese food?" Nodding I follow him in and am surprised when he is greeted warmly by the waiter. "Mr De Souza, how are you today, hungry I hope?" Stephen laughs saying, "Extremely. It's good to see you Mr Woo, how is the lovely Mrs Woo today?" The waiter smiles saying, "Busy in the kitchen as usual. You are not on your own tonight I see." He then reaches over and shakes my hand grinning happily at me. "I am pleased to see that he has a delightful companion to share his evening. My name is Mr Woo, what is your name my dear?" Smiling back I say, "Bella. I am pleased to meet

you too." Chuckling away to himself he shows us to a table in the corner. Winking he says, "Your usual table Mr De Souza. Nice and private."
Blushing I sit down in the chair that he has pulled out for me and noticing my expression Stephen laughs. "You are the first lady that I have brought here. He is probably excitedly telling his wife all about it in the kitchen as we speak." Feeling guilty for some reason I wonder what Ben would say if he knew I was having dinner with another man. I know that he wouldn't like it no matter how innocent it is. I feel a rush of adrenalin shoot through me. I hope that he does find out. Maybe then he wouldn't take me for granted like he obviously does. We order our meals and I say, "How long have you been in retail Stephen?" He looks at me for a minute before saying, "Let's not talk about work Bella. I am more interested in finding out about you. Tell me all about yourself? I laugh nervously saying, "Oh there's not much to tell really. I'm quite boring. I have lived here all of my life; after school I started working in retail and worked my way up to becoming a buyer." Looking at me thoughtfully he says, "I am sure that there is more than that to you Bella. Perhaps by the end of the meal I will have dug deeper and found out what." I don't know why but his words make me feel uncomfortable. He is looking at me carefully and it feels as if there is more

than just a casual interest in what I have to say. Mr Woo returns and we order. I decide to stick to soft drinks this evening. Not only do I have to drive home but I also feel the need to keep a clear head. Over dinner I try to find out about Stephen but like me he gives nothing away. Towards the end of the meal he leans over slightly and fixes me with an intent look saying, "So tell me Bella, how long have you and Mr Hardcastle been dating?" At the mention of Ben my heart clenches. I actually don't want to talk about him with Stephen. I am having a hard enough time as it is trying not to think about him as images of him with Vanessa come straight to the fore. Shrugging noncommittally I say, "Oh just over a year. We knew each other many years ago though and lost touch. We only met again when he bought Kinghams and the rest as they say is history."

He continues to stare at me and I feel a little uncomfortable. I decide to change the subject but before I can speak he says, "Tell me to mind my own business if you like but I am curious. Not usually being one to listen to rumours I have heard quite a few concerning you and your relationship, or should I say relationships. It appears that things weren't quite as straightforward as you imply when Mr Hardcastle, shall we say, came back into your life." Suddenly I feel angry. The last thing I want to do is talk about my personal life with him and it is none of his business. I am sure that I must look annoyed and I say abruptly, "You shouldn't listen to gossip Mr De Souza, especially a man in your position." He contemplates me a small smile tugging at the corners of his mouth. Leaning forward he says, "On the contrary Bella, I have always found gossip to be a reliable source of information and it tells me a lot about a person. Now I am intrigued as to why you are so defensive which interests me, in fact you interest me Bella. There is something lost about you which I cannot place and I have a feeling that there is a lot more going on in your life than you would have me believe."

He leans back again watching me carefully for my response. My instinct is to walk out angrily. How dare he speak to me like he has, but again something holds me back and I just merely shrug saying, "Then you will be most disappointed when you find out that my life is very normal and without drama. If you take my advice you would be better to put your energies into finding some friends outside of work. It's not healthy to eat on your own every night and it has obviously affected your overactive imagination."

Suddenly he laughs saying, "Good answer Bella. You're right it is none of my business. Maybe I will take you up on your advice, but in my experience the Good Ones, as they say are usually taken. Who knows though, maybe I

will be as lucky as Mr Hardcastle was and find love when I least expect it."
Now I feel even more uncomfortable and as our meal has finished take the opportunity to excuse myself. Trying to sound normal I smile saying, "Well it's getting late and I must be getting home. Thank you again for all of your help in the gym and for bringing me out to eat." Rummaging in my bag I take out some notes and lay them on the table. "I hope that this covers the meal, thank you again Stephen." Before I can stand however he reaches out and places his hand over mind. Looking at him in surprise he pushes the money back into it saying, "It's on me Bella. I have enjoyed your company and won't hear of you paying. If you want to return the favour though you could help me out with something at work." Pulling my hand quickly away I say, "Of course I will, just name it." He smiles and I feel uncomfortable at his expression as he says, "Tomorrow night is the Industry Awards dinner and presentation. Kinghams as you know are up for several awards one of which is Best Promotion. As this involves your department I would very much like for you to accompany me." As I hear his request it sends the blood pounding through my head and I suddenly feel light headed. I do not have a good memory of the last time I went there as I was with Ben and it was there that I discovered about Nathan and

Ben's double life. Everything unravelled for me that night and the memory is still painful. I can feel him watching my reaction with interest and I stutter saying, "I don't know. I mean Ben wouldn't like it if I went without him and thinking about it I can't make tomorrow." I know that he will see through my excuses in an instant but even I am surprised when he says in a steely voice, "Nonsense. Ben wouldn't care as it is your job. Any plans that you have you can change. I am sure that Ben wouldn't expect you to sit in every night waiting for him to return. You would be doing me a favour as your boss and I for one would welcome spending an evening with someone who doesn't want me to take them home with me at the end of it." I am shocked by his arrogance. No wonder he is alone if he has such a high opinion of himself. His words about me waiting in every night though strike a chord within me. Ben obviously isn't, judging by the rumours of his evening activities with Vanessa, so I decide that two can play at that game and I won't as Stephen says, just wait around for Ben to return. Maybe an innocent evening out with someone else is just what I need right now. Ben can't complain as it is work related anyway. Staring back at Stephen I say, "Ok then. You're right. I should go with you, it's the least I can do after your help this evening." A small triumphant expression flashes across his face and then he stands saying, "Good. That's all sorted then. I will pick you up at 6.30pm. Dress to impress as they say." In alarm I reply, "No need for that. I'll meet you there." Shaking his head he says, "Absolutely not. I will not having you travelling to and from London on your own late at night."

The last thing I want is for him to come to the house so I say, "No need to come and get me. I will bring my things and change at work. Then we can go from there. It will save time and we can get the train and avoid the traffic."

Stephen looks at me with interest and then merely smiles saying, "Ok, let's do it your way. Come on, I'll walk you to your car."

After paying the bill and saying our goodbyes to Mr Woo, Stephen walks with me to my car. We talk about mundane things and as we reach it I turn to him and smile. "Well, that was an unexpected evening. Thank you again for everything. Can I offer you a lift?" He shifts slightly and I am suddenly aware that he has moved closer to me and I feel the hard metal of the car on my back as I press against it. Speaking softly he says, "No thank you. I have my car nearby. Take care of yourself Bella driving home. Make sure that you get some sleep and drinks lots of water. You are probably still dehydrated and I need you back in tip top condition for our evening out tomorrow."

I am glad that it is dark as I can feel myself blushing as I feel his scrutiny. He is so close and I can feel his breath on my face. Feeling extremely uncomfortable I cough nervously saying, "Ok, well good night Stephen. Thank you again and I'll see you tomorrow." As he turns to walk away I say quickly, "Oh, and for your information I finished the report that you asked for. I will look forward to hearing your comments." He flashes me a wicked grin and says, "I am very much looking forward to reading it. There's always room for improvement Bella, in every aspect of life. Sometimes you don't even realise that it is needed until the opportunity presents itself to you."

He heads off and as I watch him go I feel uncomfortable again. He wasn't talking about the report, that much I could tell. Feeling uneasy I wonder what his agenda is. There is definitely something more to him than meets the eye.

Chapter 15

On getting home I look around me at the large empty house. All the life left it when Ben went away and now it depresses me to return to its emptiness every night. Sighing to myself I decide to run a nice deep bath and try to relax.
As I lay there soaking in the sweet scented water I feel my body relaxing. I totally overdid it at the gym and I can already feel my body groaning in protest at my treatment of it. I can't believe that I allowed myself to get so wound up. My evening with Stephen was also a surprise. He intrigues me and I feel totally on edge around him. I can't work him out and there is a danger to him which screams at me to avoid him at all costs. I have never met anyone as arrogant as he is and then images of Ben replace the ones I have of Stephen and my eyes fill up once again. I can't believe how much I miss him. It wouldn't be so bad but I can't get the picture out of my mind of him and Vanessa.
Once I have dried myself and changed into my pyjamas I head off downstairs to make myself a drink.
As I pass Ben's study I decide that I will have my drink in there. Once it is made I take it with me and as I push

open the door I inhale the distinct aroma of his space. The room smells of Ben. The smell of leather and polished wood mingle with traces of his aftershave. I sink down into his leather chair and allow it to envelop me as I imagine that the chair is Ben's arms holding me tightly, keeping me safe and reassuring me.

I know that I shouldn't but I flick his computer on. Against my better judgement I once again start searching for information about Vanessa. I study the images looking for any that include Ben. I know that I am torturing myself but it is as if I am on a path of self destruction. By the end of the evening I have built up quite an understanding of her life. I discover that her husband Claude committed suicide and there are pictures of his funeral at which Vanessa cuts a striking figure dressed all in black with dark glasses on. As I study the pictures I suddenly see a familiar face in the crowd of mourners. I can see Ben watching Vanessa with a worried expression. He appears to be on his own and is standing some way from her but I can tell that he is on edge as he looks towards her.

I knew that he worked there at the time so it is not unusual for him to be there but there is something about his expression that makes me think that there is more to it.

Intrigued I search for articles about Claude's death. The

general consensus of opinion was that he shot himself to avoid the humiliation that his actions contributed to the banking crisis. There are many reports about his dodgy dealings and many unfavourable comparisons between him and his predecessor Vanessa's father, who was apparently a banking genius who built the bank up to where it was before the collapse.

I also read with interest in the gossip columns about Vanessa and her meltdown. I can understand why she folded as accompanying the reports are ones of her husband with speculation about his affairs and the state of their marriage. Then my investigations bring me more up to date. Since her husband's death over two years ago Vanessa hasn't been seen with anyone else. There are a string of pictures of her at various events always accompanied by gorgeous men, but there is never the same one twice and I can tell that there is no closeness between any of them, that is until the one that I come to again of the one with her and Ben.

In the privacy of his study once again I study the picture. They are not stated as being together but it is obvious to me that they share a closeness that is missing from all the other pictures. I know every inch of Ben's face and recognise his expression. Her eyes are brimming with happiness and she looks more animated and alive in this picture than any of the others that I have seen. Shutting down the computer I have no wish to delve anymore. Everything that I fear is in that picture. Well I am not going to stay here waiting for his call anymore. It is time to fight back against his former life. One thing is certain; I can't live with someone who has another life outside of the one with me. First thing tomorrow I am calling Pete and demanding that he gets Ben to call me.

Chapter 16

When the morning comes around I groan as I wake up and take in the fact that I can hardly move. Easing myself slowly out of bed I set about getting ready. Realising that I need to pack a bag for later I decide on what to wear. Instantly I see the red dress that Ben bought me for the same occasion last year. I had been so excited to wear it and had felt like a million dollars. The evening had ended in disaster and I haven't worn it since. Tonight however I feel different. I feel as though I need to get some control over my own life and it may as well start with burying a few demons. Decision made I pack the dress with matching underwear and shoes and once I am ready head off to work.

I see Karen on my way in and in a low tone she tells me of her meeting with Stephen that preceded the one that I had with him. It was the same as mine and she says, "All day it took me to compile the report. Imogen was off so I had to do it all myself. I was late home and in a really bad mood with the children. I am dreading today. What if he finds fault with what I have done?" Looking at her sympathetically I say, "I know. Luckily for me April helped me. I handed it in on my way to the gym and then you'll never guess what happened." Karen looks at me with interest saying, "No, tell me." I then tell her all about my evening and by the end of it her eyes are as wide as saucers. "Oh my God, you poor thing. That is rotten luck. What do you think that Ben would say if he knew that you spent the evening with our charismatic new tyrant?" I laugh it off saying, "Well as he put him here in the first place then he only has himself to blame." Karen looks at me sympathetically and says, "I know that he is away at the moment, have you heard from him, will he be back soon?" Feeling my face fall I reply, "No and I don't know when he will be back. In fact I am going to try and speak to him today to find out." Karen squeezes my arm in sympathy and then says, "Oh my God, look at the time. Do you fancy having lunch with me later and we can catch up then?" I nod and we arrange to meet in the staff canteen at 1pm.

As I head off to my office I resolve to ring Pete before I do anything else. Luckily April isn't in yet so I seize the opportunity and make the much needed call. Pete answers after the first ring saying, "Hi Bella. It's good to hear from you. What can I help you with?" My voice shaking slightly I say, "I'm sorry to trouble you Pete but I was wondering if you could get a message to Ben asking him to call me?" There is a slight pause and then Pete says gently. "I'm sorry to ask Bella, but can you tell me what it's about? My instructions are not to call him unless it's an emergency." My insides scream out at me with frustration. It's an emergency to me but I know that it won't be seen as such to Pete. Swallowing hard I say, "Well it's not an emergency as such, I just need to know when he is coming home." Once again there is a brief pause and then Pete says, "I don't know Bella, I haven't been told. Listen if there is anything I can help you with you only have to ask. I am sure that it won't be much longer now." I can feel the tears welling up as I hear the sympathy in his voice. Blinking rapidly I say, "Oh it's nothing really. I am just struggling a bit with the radio silence that's all." Pete replies, "I know, it must be hard for you. I know that it is for him too. Unfortunately though he has a job to do and must see it through. Stay strong Bella, he'll be back before you know it." Sighing I say, "Thanks Pete. I'm sorry to have troubled you." "Anytime Bella, and I mean that." I put the phone down and once again feel empty inside. The call has achieved nothing and I am no further forward knowing what is happening. In a way I am glad that I am going out tonight. Maybe it is just what the doctor ordered. Feeling despondent I turn on my computer and start working. April soon comes in and the day begins. I soon see an e mail from Stephen calling a manager's meeting at 11.00am which annoys me. He hasn't even checked to see if we have any appointments. I am almost tempted to e mail back saying I can't make it but then again it is better not to rock the boat. I mention it to April and she looks worried saying, "I hope that it's not bad news. I wouldn't put anything past him." Agreeing with her inside I merely say, "Oh it's probably nothing. I'll let you know if it's anything bad." We carry on with our work and I am dreading 11.00 coming.

The dreaded hour soon arrives and I find myself sitting next to Karen waiting for the meeting to begin. Our fellow managers are sitting around looking equally despondent, waiting for Stephen to start. He in turn looks totally relaxed. Looking around the room he calls everyone to attention.

"Thank you all for coming at such short notice. I hope that I didn't inconvenience you in any way." There is a general murmur and he carries on. "As you are all now aware I am dissatisfied with the level of business that we are currently operating at and it needs to improve." I notice that everyone looks uncomfortable and extremely put out. As a store we are currently running at 5% up which given the market conditions I think is acceptable. However Stephen obviously doesn't think so and carries on. "By now I have all of your reports on my desk which I will read and then set up meetings individually with you all. In the meantime though I want you to think hard about ways in which we can improve things. Don't bother coming to the meeting if you haven't got at least five suggestions on how we can go about this. I will e mail each one of you with the time of the meeting and I expect you all to have done your homework. There is no room for complacency here and I do not tolerate fools gladly. Right now, does anyone have any questions?" Looking around I can see the faces of my fellow managers. Nobody looks happy and due to the tone of Stephen's voice I very much doubt if anyone has anything to say, at least to his face. When nobody speaks he says, "Good, right then off you go and I will be in touch."

Everyone scrambles to their feet, not wanting to stay in the room a minute more than they have to, me included. However before I can leave he says, "Bella, please stay behind, I need a word." Karen raises her eyes up and looks at me sympathetically. "I'll see you at 1 for lunch." She says in a whisper and I nod miserably.

The room empties and Stephen says, "How are you feeling today Bella, I expect that you ache?" Surprised I smile saying, "Yes I do. It's my own fault though." He laughs and says, "Yes you could say that. Have you taken anything for it?" Shaking my head I reply, "No, but I'll be fine, thank you for your concern." He goes into his drawer and takes out a small packet of tablets.

"Here, have two Ibuprofen. They should help with any inflammation. I can't have you fading on me later." Taking them from him I am actually quite grateful. "Thank you Stephen. I'm sure that I will be fine." He considers me for a moment and then says. "Anyway, I wanted to say don't bother changing here. I have arranged for the use of a room at the hotel before the event. That way you won't have to wear your best dress on the train. Just bring your bag and meet me outside the staff entrance at 6pm."

Feeling a little awkward I just smile and he says, "Ok then off you go. I don't want to keep you from your work." He then turns back abruptly to his computer and I quickly make my exit.

When I meet up with Karen later I tell her what he said. Laughing she says, "Oh my God, that is so awkward. You poor thing. Not only do you have to make polite conversation with him on the journey but then you have to share a room with him when you get there." She shrieks with laughter and I pretend to be annoyed. "Stop laughing. You know we aren't sharing a room. We will probably just take it in turns. It's not an ideal situation to be in but I didn't have much choice. I just hope that there are some better people to talk to on our table otherwise it will be a long night." Once again Karen laughs saying, "Well I'll think of you whilst I'm watching Coronation

Street with my feet up. You must tell me everything tomorrow though, and don't leave anything out." Thankfully we leave this subject behind and talk about other non related work things for the rest of our break. The day passes by fairly quickly and I soon find myself waiting for Stephen at the staff entrance. I still ache, despite the tablets, and could really do with just going home and having a warm bath. I don't have to wait for long and soon see Stephen striding towards me bag in hand. As he draws near he winks and says, "All set for our night on the town." I smile but notice the surprised look of the security guard on the desk by the door. Blushing I look away. It will be all round the store tomorrow and even though it is an innocent work related event I know how people love to gossip. Stephen laughs as he sees my discomfort and noticing my bag says, "Here let me carry your bag for you." Shaking my head I say, "Oh its fine. It's not heavy, in fact it has wheels so don't worry." Ignoring me he takes it from me. "Nonsense, it will balance mine out. Come on otherwise we will miss the train." Flinging an anguished look towards the security guard he smiles as I reluctantly follow Stephen out of the door. He strides along at quite a pace and thankfully I don't have to say much, just concentrate on keeping up with him. We are soon on a train bound for London and gratefully I sink back into the seat. Looking at me with concern Stephen says, "Still aching?" I nod miserably and he says, "We'll pick up some more tablets at the other end. You'll never get through the evening otherwise." Thinking that he is probably right I smile saying, "Thank you. Yes they do help a bit. I think that I'll give the gym a rest for a while though." Arching his eyebrows he says, "It's not the gym that's the problem. It's people who don't know what they're doing that are. Next time you should take advantage of their Instructors who will work out a programme for you to follow." I nod and then look out of the window. I'm not up to a lecture from him about the dos and don'ts of attending the gym.

Thankfully the carriage is fairly empty despite it being rush hour. Most people are coming out of London and not going into it. Our conversation is minimal and Stephen spends most of the journey answering e mails on his phone.

We are soon there and once we are through the barriers he drags me to a nearby shop. "Come on we'll get you some tablets in here." He waits whilst I pay and we then get a cab to the hotel.

The event is in a fabulous hotel that is very grand. Under different circumstances I would be excited to spend time here. I remember the last time I came here with Ben and I wish with all my heart that he was with me now.

Stephen goes to the reception and comes back with a key to a room. Here you go Bella; we can get ready in here. Handing me the key he says, "You go first and I'll be up in half an hour. Unless you need longer, I know what you women are like." Feeling irritated I almost snatch the key from him and say, "No, half an hour will be fine thank you." Nodding he says, "Ok, I'll do some work down here and then I'll be up."

Grateful for some time to myself I find the room. It is a lovely room that under different circumstances I would be excited to be in. Conscious of the time I have a quick shower and get dressed. As I put the red dress on I have flashbacks to when I wore it last. Ben had bought it for me and I had felt like a Princess. Holding back the tears I apply my make up and as I brush my hair there is a knock on the door. With a sinking feeling I open it to see Stephen waiting to come in. As he sees me I notice his eyes flash and a smile breaks out across his face. "You look amazing Bella. What's the saying? Oh yes, you scrub up well." Lowering my eyes I walk back into the room. "Thank you. Anyway, your turn now. I'll just grab my bag and leave you in peace." Following me inside he says, "That's fine. I wouldn't expect you to hang around downstairs just take a seat and I'll be as quick as I can." He notices as I shake my head and before I can reply says, "Just sit down Bella. Take your tablets and flick on

the TV. Try to relax, I won't be long."
Sighing I do as he says and watch the news whilst I wait. It feels strange to be in a hotel room with another man and I can't say that I am enjoying the experience. Ben would freak out if he knew, I think with a small amount of satisfaction. I wonder where he is now. London is actually quite a small place and the thought that he may not be far away just increases my longing for him.
As I wait for Stephen to get ready I think back over the day. Karen and I had a great lunch where we had a good old moan about him. She was appalled to think that I had to spend the evening with him and made me laugh when she said that she was glad that her department hadn't won anything otherwise it may have been her standing here in my place. I am not sure why but for some reason I think that this event is just an excuse.

Interrupting my thoughts Stephen comes out of the bathroom. I notice how striking he looks in a black dinner jacket. The smell of his aftershave mingles with the soap from the shower and his hair is still damp. He smiles saying, "We are still a bit early, would you like to get a drink or we could just stay here if you would prefer?" I jump up awkwardly saying, "No a drink would be fine thank you." I can feel him studying me and pretend to be busy gathering my things. As I turn to face him he says softly, "Ben is a lucky man Bella. If I was him I wouldn't leave you alone for a minute." Feeling completely thrown off guard I look at him in shock. I can feel my face blushing and he smiles noticing my discomfort. "I am sorry, I didn't intend on embarrassing you. Come on, I'll buy you a drink." Leaving our belongings behind we head off downstairs. It feels strange walking next to him and when we enter the lift I am glad to see that we are not the sole occupants. There is an older couple in there already who smile at us as we enter. The man winks at me and says, "Good evening." We both return the greeting and as the lift closes he says, "What a striking couple you make. You are a lucky man," he says turning to Stephen. The woman also smiles saying, "Don't embarrass them Henry." Turning to me she says, "He's always had an eye for a pretty girl. It's been a lifetime's work keeping him in check." He chuckles and grabs hold of her hand. "There's only ever been one girl for me Stella. You know that, I thank my lucky stars every day that I married you." Stephen grins at me and I grin back at him. Despite the fact that they have misjudged our relationship we don't put them right. It doesn't matter and I enjoy watching the two of them together. I pray with all my heart that Ben and I will be as much as love with each other when we are their age.

Once we are downstairs we go to the bar for a drink. I opt for a glass of red wine and look with interest around me. There are all sorts of people here. Some are dressed in their business suits and are busily working away on their computers. Others are chatting over drinks, possibly going out to the theatre. There aren't many as dressed up as we are which makes us the subject of many an interested look. I notice a group of women excitedly eyeing Stephen up and when he returns with the drinks I nod my head towards them saying, "Looks like you have a fan club over there." He looks at them and they giggle amongst themselves. Grinning at me he says, "Not in your league Bella. Like I said before Ben's a lucky man." Once again I blush as red as my dress and he laughs saying, "Are you always this easy to wind up?" Laughing I say, "Actually yes. Ben has always enjoyed winding me up because he knows how easily I am embarrassed." I notice with surprise that as I mention Ben's name a flash of irritation passes across his face. It goes as quickly as it came and as he hands me my drink he smiles and says, "I think that this is going to be a long night."

We don't have long to wait before I recognise some of the managers from our other stores. They come over and

I introduce them to Stephen. There is soon quite a crowd of us and I enjoy talking to my colleagues from the different branches. They ask about Ben and I just repeat that he is away on business. They don't ask much more than that so it is easy to brush their questions aside. There is soon quite a crowd of us. The Hardcastle group have eight stores and so we have reserved three tables for the evening. I am hoping that I will get to sit with my fellow buyers. It may help with the boredom that is inevitable at such occasions.

I spend most of the time chatting to my fellow homewares buyer from the Kingston store. We compare notes and she is very good company. After a while she lowers her voice saying, "What's the story with your new manager?" Surprised I say, "What do you mean, story?"

She looks towards him and then turning away from his direction she says, "He hasn't taken his eyes off you the whole time we have been talking. If I didn't know better I would say that he is interested in you and not just as colleagues either." She has totally shocked me and without turning around to look at him I say, "Of course he's not. He knows that I have a boyfriend." Laughing wryly she says, "Does he know who your boyfriend is? I mean if he does then he is playing a dangerous game." Nodding I say, "Yes he does. I am sure you are mistaken though. He is probably just watching me in case I do something to embarrass him or the store." Shaking her head she says, "No, I know that look. Although I wish it was directed at me, he's gorgeous." Pulling a face I say, "Well looks won over personality in his case. Be careful what you wish for, he is a nightmare to work with." Before she can comment further there is an announcement that we should all take our places for the evening's event. We are to have dinner first and then the awards ceremony will take place.

Vowing to stick close to my colleague I follow her into the event.

Chapter 17

Before I can sit next to Ellen, Stephen calls to me from the next table. "Over here Bella, our table is this one." Ellen laughs at my expression and her expression says - I told you so. Annoyed I go over to where he is holding a chair out for me. As I sit down he pushes the chair in and as he sits down next to me he leans over and whispers, "There, now I can keep an eye on you." As I look at him in surprise he laughs and says, "I can tell that you're still aching. It's written all over your face. I've got some more tablets on me if you need them."

I can't believe that he can tell how uncomfortable I am. He is right though, I am well and truly suffering now and the thought of some pain killers is a welcome thought. Gratefully I say, "Actually I could do with some. The last lot have worn off already. How many can I take in a 24 hour period?" Grinning he says, "Eight. You could probably take two more now and two when you get home." Thanking him I wash the tablets down with some water and curse the day that I thought the gym was a good idea.

Luckily one of the other buyers is next to me on the other side and we chat happily about work and holidays. Soon the meal comes which is quite nice considering the amount of people that need feeding. There is also a lot to drink but I try to stick to water, due to the tablets that I have taken. I also feel the need to keep a clear head. The last thing I want is to be drunk around Ben's employees. Soon the meal is over and the awards ceremony begins. I look around me with interest at the various recipients of the awards. The Hardcastle group fare quite well and receive two awards. One for Best Department Store in the South East and one for Best Window Display in the Bromley Store. It all seems to drag on forever. Stephen is actually quite good company and keeps me amused with his cutting remarks about the other stores and various people going up to receive the awards.

Half way through I feel the need to escape to the ladies. This slightly worries me as I didn't have such a good experience the last time that I went. However, everything seems different this time and I feel the need to stretch my legs. Whispering to Stephen that I am going he turns and holds on to my arm pulling me nearer to him. He whispers, "You wouldn't get me a drink would you Bella? I'm sick of wine and could murder a brandy." He takes some notes out of his wallet and says, "Get one for yourself too. For medicinal purposes." He grins at me and laughing I say, "Ok, no problem. Should I ask the others?" He nods in agreement and I ask the rest of the table if they want anything. Nobody takes us up on it so I head off in search of the ladies and then the bar.

It feels good to stretch my legs and I go in search of the rest rooms. I remember back to the last time I used them. Ben's boss told me about Nathan's crime and Ben's secret job. By the end of our conversation I had found myself agreeing to leave Ben and go back to Nathan. My heart clenches when I remember how I felt. Such a lot has happened since and despite the current circumstances I do trust Ben and have never been happier. Luckily there is no such meeting this time and I am soon heading off in search of the bar.

It appears quite busy so I wait patiently for my turn. There is a different crowd in here now than earlier and they are more dressed up and the atmosphere is lively and loud.

I find it interesting to watch what is going on around me and after about ten minutes I get to the front of the bar. I place my order and whilst I wait I notice two attractive ladies push in next to me. Shifting over I can't help but hear their conversation as they are talking to each other loudly over the noise from the bar.

"Why is it so busy in here tonight?" One of then says to the other. "Oh some awards ceremony I think, something to do with the retail sector."

"Oh yes, come to think about it my friend was due to

come here but cancelled at the last minute." Her friend shouts, "Who, do I know them?" Laughing the girl replies, "Yes, it's Vanessa." "What Vanessa Montague?" she says incredulously. Suddenly I am all ears. The girl nods and her friend carries on. "What on earth has she got to do with the retail sector, other than keeping it going through these difficult times?" They both dissolve into laughter. My drinks have arrived but I am not going anywhere. I want to hear what they say next. Taking a sip I try to look as though I am going to make a call. "Well, she cancelled due to her boyfriend. Apparently he owns several department stores and didn't want to come. She said that he finds these things boring and would rather spend the night in bed with her." Suddenly I feel faint. They carry on. "Oh, is this the one she has been with for a few years now. Didn't he go away for a bit though?" Her friend nods and says, "Yes, apparently he had some business to see to. But now he's back and they are certainly making up for lost time if you know what I mean." Her friend laughs saying, "I don't blame her. Have you seen him, he's the total package. I wouldn't want to go out either if I was her." The waiter interrupts them and they order their drinks. Their conversation turns to other things and I am left devastated.

Pushing back through the bar I am unaware of the noise and crowd around me. Their words keep on repeating themselves in my brain. My legs feel weak and I sink down on to a nearby chair. All of my worst fears are coming true. I don't understand it. I know that Ben is doing a job but the girl's words haunt me and I wonder if I was just a job and he was telling the same thing to Vanessa. It must be true because otherwise why would they be talking about it. The image of them together in the photograph enters my mind and I am in total shock. I take hold of the Brandy and down it in one. I need something to steady my nerves.

I am unaware of anything around me and just replay the conversation over and over in my mind. Somebody pushes past me and I am brought back to reality. Taking the other Brandy I head off back to the room. All I want to do is go home but I am not going to make a scene like the last time. The evening will soon be over and I will think about it all when I get back.

I return to the table and Stephen looks at me in surprise. "You were ages. Is everything alright?" Mustering a smile that I don't feel I say, "Yes it's fine, sorry there was a long queue that took ages." He stares at me and I can tell that he knows that something is wrong but he doesn't push it and I just sit down next to him and try to concentrate on what is going on. This however is more easily said than done. My mind is buzzing with what I have just heard. As if on auto pilot I carry on. I don't even register that I am drinking wine until Stephen leans over saying, "I think you've had enough Bella. Remember you're on tablets." I look at him in confusion and suddenly realise that I feel very unwell indeed. He pours me a large glass of water and in a stern voice says, "Drink this." As I empty the glass he whispers, "Right no more alcohol. As soon as this is finished I'm taking you home."

I sit quietly for the rest of the evening. Luckily we don't win the award so I am spared the ordeal of going up to receive it. As the evening draws to a close everyone makes their way outside. However as soon as we exit the room I start to feel really sick. Without saying anything I make a mad dash for the ladies and just reach it in time. I am violently sick and I can't appear to stop. I don't even care if anyone can hear me. Tears run down my face as I retch continuously into the toilet.

I am not even sure how long I am in here for. I can't stop retching even though there is nothing else left. I feel so weak and can't move from my position sitting on the floor. I can hear voices outside but it is just those of people going about their business. Suddenly I hear someone shout, "You can't come in here." Then I hear the unmistakeable sound of Stephen's voice sounding angry. "I don't care, move out of my way." Then I hear him shout, "Bella, are you ok, where are you?" The ladies voice says, "I'm calling someone." I hear him obviously knocking on all the doors and I say weakly, "I'm in this one. Wait a minute." Dragging myself up I unlock the door. Stephen rushes in and in one fell swoop gathers me up in his arms and strides out of the toilets. I feel too surprised to say anything and he doesn't stop until we are back in the room that we changed in earlier. Carefully he sits me down on the bed and sinking on to his heels he sits in front of me holding on to my hands. There is concern in his face as he says, "Don't worry Bella. I think that it must be the pills reacting to the alcohol. Here lay down and I will get you some water." I do as he says as I am too weak to care about the situation. As I lay my head on the pillow I close my eyes to shut out the nightmare that has unfolded. Almost immediately I feel Stephen lifting my head up gently and holding a cup of water to my lips. "Here drink this. It will help make you feel better." Tears slide down my face and I say weakly, "I'm so sorry Stephen. You shouldn't have to deal with all of this." Crouching beside me he says, "Hush now Bella. Don't worry about me. I'm kind of getting used to what a night out with you involves." As I look at him he winks and then he pushes my hair back from my face. "Why don't you sleep it off Bella? I will go downstairs and organise the room for the night. You are in no fit state to travel anywhere." I look

at him in alarm and try to sit up. "Oh no I'll be ok in a minute. Don't worry." Gently he pushes me back down. "Nonsense, I insist." Then he looks at me with a concerned expression and says, "I feel partly responsible for this. I should have insisted that you had no alcohol at all." I shake my head saying, "It's not your fault Stephen." Still looking concerned he says, "Would you like me to call Ben?" On hearing his name the tears start to fall and wiping them quickly away I say, "No you can't reach him. He is away." Before he can answer I feel as if I am going to be sick again and pull myself up and make a dash for the bathroom. I just make it in time and then slump to the floor. I notice that my dress is covered and I feel ashamed. I can't believe the state I am in. Surely it can't be the Ibuprofen, it must be a bug.
I hear knocking on the door and Stephen says, "Are you ok in there?" Mustering as much normality in my voice as I can I answer, "I'm fine thank you. I just need a minute." He replies, "Well if you're sure. I'll just go and sort out a room and then I'll be back with fresh supplies of water." I hear the door close and I drag myself up and look in the mirror.
The sight that greets me is not a pleasant one. My make up is streaked all down my face and there is vomit in my hair. My dress is covered and I smell disgusting. I can't believe that Stephen has seen me like this and despite it

not being my fault I feel ashamed. Tearing off the dress I throw it into the corner. That dress is bad luck. I never want to wear it again. I quickly run the shower and as I stand underneath the hot jets my tears join the stream as it cleanses my body. I stand there for ages and then reluctantly turn it off and wrap myself in a towel. Once I am dry I lift the complimentary hotel robe from the back of the door and wrap myself in it. When I go back into the room I can see that I am alone. Grateful for the solitude I sink down on to the bed and curl up into the foetal position. As I lie there all I can think of is Ben. Images of him with Vanessa haunt me as I drift off into a troubled sleep.

Chapter 18

I wake up to a banging sound. In confusion I open my eyes and look around. The unfamiliar sight of the hotel room swims into view and I realise that the banging is coming from inside my head. Groaning I raise my hand up in a futile attempt to stop it.
Suddenly a voice says, "Morning Bella, how are you feeling?" Looking towards the sound I am horrified to see Stephen sitting in the chair by the window looking very uncomfortable. He has obviously been there all night given the sight of him. He looks tired and dishevelled and there is stubble on his chin and his eyes look red with lack of sleep. Gingerly I pull myself up to face him, conscious that I am in nothing more than the hotel dressing gown. In confusion I say, "What happened?"
Grinning at me he says, "What you can't remember?" As he sees my expression he laughs saying, "Don't worry. You had a bad reaction to the tablets that you took and were violently sick. By the time I came back with fresh supplies of water you were out cold and I couldn't wake you." Feeling confused I say, "Have you been here all night?" Nodding he says, "Yes, unfortunately the hotel is

full and there were no more rooms available so I slept in this chair." As he shifts in the chair he grimaces. "It would appear that I need the Ibuprofen now though. It wasn't very comfortable." I suddenly feel terrible. He looks as if he has had the worst night of his life and it is all down to me. Looking at him sitting there I feel extremely grateful to him. "I'm sorry Stephen. You must regret asking me now. If it wasn't for me you would have had a great evening and be sleeping in the comfort of your own home." He smiles, which I notice lights up his face. I think to myself that he should smile more as it totally changes him. I am so used to his stern, scowling expression that I missed what a nice guy he can be. "Bella, don't apologise, it wasn't your fault. These things happen, although it would appear that you get your fair share of drama." I laugh and instantly regret it as my head bangs back at me in anger. Wincing I say, "I wish that this headache would go." Stephen jumps up and grabs a bottle of water from the table. "Here, drink this. It's probably better to stay off the tablets but the water will help." Gratefully I take a sip and he says, "If it's ok with you Bella I think that I'll have a shower to revive me. I won't be long and then you can get ready." "Oh, that's fine. Go ahead I'll just sit here and try to return to normality." Laughing he says, "Yes, it was quite a night. Although usually when I spend a night with a beautiful lady I don't spend it crumpled up in a chair all night watching her sleep." He goes off to the bathroom leaving me feeling mortified. The thought of him watching me sleep makes me uncomfortable. I hope that he was just joking.

As I sit there alone I think about Ben and Vanessa. I can't believe what I overheard last night and have absolutely no reason to suspect that it isn't true. It even sounded like Ben. He told me that he hated the Awards ceremonies and would rather just be in bed with me. I feel numb and a growing sense of anger is building up inside of me. I have had enough of waiting for him to finish his secret job. As soon as I get home I am calling Pete and I am not going to be fobbed off this time. I need answers before I am driven mad.

Just then there is a loud knock on the door. The noise just makes my head hurt even more and Stephen comes out of the bathroom with a towel wrapped around his waist.

"I'll get it Bella, don't move." He opens the door and I hear him say, "Thank you. Just bring it in and put it on the table." Looking up in confusion I see a waiter carrying a silver tray laden with breakfast items. He nods at me and says, "Good morning Madam." He then places the tray on the table and scurries away. I look at Stephen in confusion and he says, "I thought that you wouldn't

be up to a full English this morning so I ordered us a continental breakfast last night. You need to eat something and can probably only manage something light." Feeling bewildered I say, "Thank you, Stephen. I'm not sure that I can eat anything though." Raising his eyes up he says, "Nonsense. I insist even if it's just a small mouthful of toast."
Grabbing the tray he brings it over to the bed and places it between us, sitting next to me. I avert my eyes as I feel embarrassed to be in such intimate proximity to him. He is obviously naked with just a towel covering his modesty. His body is well toned and very muscular and is still glistening with droplets of water from the shower. Nervously I laugh saying, "Well this isn't awkward is it?" Taking a mouthful of croissant he just winks at me wickedly. When he has finished he says, "What do you think Ben would say if he could see you now." Flushing at the mention of Ben I say, "Well he wouldn't like it. That much is certain. Although it is very innocent I am sure the thought of me in bed with a naked man is not a pleasant one." Laughing he says, "I agree. If it was me in his position I would want to kill him, innocent or not." Taking a piece of toast I eat it slowly. Then I say, "What about you Stephen, have you got a girlfriend?" Shaking his head he says ruefully, "No, nobody special. I am not short of female company though if that's what you

mean, there's just been nobody special that I have wanted to settle down with." He fixes me with a steady gaze and says, "All of the good ones are already taken. Although I live in hope that things may change and then I will seize my chance."

Looking away quickly I feel really awkward now. He is so compelling and the intimacy of our situation is starting to make me even more uncomfortable than I was already.

Coughing slightly I say, "You wouldn't be able to pass me an orange juice would you Stephen? I feel quite thirsty now." "Of course I will." He leans over and hands me the glass. As he does his fingers brush against mine and I almost drop the glass in shock. Still staring at me a slow smile spreads across his face. "Come on drink up. I'll finish getting ready and then when you are I'll take you home."

Trying not to appear flustered I gulp the drink down and say, "Thanks, after last night I think a day of recovery is long overdue."

He goes back into the bathroom and I quickly take the opportunity to throw on the clothes that I wore yesterday. I will have a shower when I get home. The sooner I get out of here the better.

Chapter 19

I have never been so glad to get home. As I approach the gates the relief is overwhelming. The journey home was fairly quiet. Stephen didn't say much which I was grateful for. I still feel dreadful and I think that he could tell that I wasn't up to chatting. He was quite sweet really. He insisted on carrying my bag to my car and had looked concerned asking me if I wanted him to drop me off home, instead of driving myself. I assured him that I would be ok and thanked him for all of his help.
Luckily I am off for two days which should give me enough time to recover. I certainly have a lot to think about. The conversation that I overheard keeps on playing around and around in my mind. I think that it is driving me mad and as soon as I get in I am phoning Pete.
Once I get inside I drop my bag on the floor of the hallway and wander into the kitchen. All of a sudden I get the shock of my life because there sitting in front of me is Ben's boss and Pete. Looking at them in horror I notice a wry smile on his boss's face.
"What's this Bella, the walk of shame?" she says and laughs. Pete looks embarrassed and I look at them both

in confusion. She adds, "It must have been a good night judging by your appearance." Collecting my thoughts I am suddenly worried. "What is it, is it Ben is he alright?" I say anxiously. Shaking her head she says, "No Ben is fine, it's you we've come to see." She watches me intently and I sink down on to the settee. "Me? What on earth do you want to talk to me for, and how did you get in?" Leaning forward she says, "We have quite a lot to talk to you about and we let ourselves in with the key." I look at Pete and he looks kindly at me. "I'm sorry Bella; this must be quite a shock for you. In fact you don't look so well, are you ok?" Nodding I say, "I'm fine thank you, but please just tell me what's going on." Ben's boss looks at Pete and says, "Make us all a drink Pete would you? I could do with one and Bella certainly looks like she could." Pulling a face at her behind her back Pete sets about making the coffee. Leaning forward she says, "I am interested in what happened to you last night Bella. I understand that you went to the awards ceremony with a certain Stephen De Souza. Tell me everything that happened." I feel shocked. Why on earth would she be interested in that, enough to make a special trip here? I tell them all about it and she looks puzzled. "So from what you are telling me, you had too many tablets that reacted badly with the alcohol and you ended up sleeping it off at the hotel." I nod, taking the coffee that Pete offers me gratefully. Ben's boss looks at me sharply and says, "Right then. Now tell me everything you haven't told me. I want to know every detail no matter how small. Firstly tell me everything about Stephen. How you met, how often you have met and anything that he has told you about himself." Feeling even more confused I tell them everything I know. I add that he is difficult to work with but was extremely kind to me both at the gym and last night. They look at one another thoughtfully and then Pete says, "What happened at the bar?" Once again I am shocked. I haven't mentioned the bar incident and how do they even know that I went to the bar? "How do you know about that?" I say incredulously. Ben's boss smiles and says, "Because we were watching you Bella. Something happened at the bar and then you unravelled. I have a feeling that you didn't like something you heard. We watched you knock the alcohol back after that so I am thinking that it was something concerning Ben, am I right?" I just look at her in amazement. I can't believe that they were watching me. Why on earth would they?

Pete looks at me sympathetically. "Bella, certain information has come to light that Ben's operation is not as straightforward as we thought. Once again it all points back to you and we need to get to the bottom of it. Any help that you could give us at this point would help us enormously. Please tell us everything, no matter how insignificant it may seem." Sinking back in my chair I lean back, my head against the cushion. My head is throbbing and I can't take it all in. Maybe I am just a job to Ben. I don't know how but it is all too much. I can feel the ever present tears welling up in my eyes and Ben's boss looks at me in exasperation. "Cut out the emotion Bella, I am only interested in the facts." Her words shock me and I can see Pete look away in embarrassment.

In dull tones I tell them what I heard. They look confused and I notice that they share a puzzled look. Ben's boss says, "Why on earth would they say that?" Crossly I say, "Probably because it is true. They didn't know who I was so it must be." Ben's boss leans in towards me and says sternly, "Of course they knew it was you. Open your eyes Bella; you have been set up from the start. It's a classic case. But what I want to know is why?" Turning to Pete she says briskly, "Find out everything you can on this Stephen de Souza. Study the CCTV at the gym and the hotel. Put a tag on him and report back anything you find. Delve into his past and find out how he got the job. Turning back towards me she says, "Pull yourself together Bella and start thinking clearly and logically. Anything that you can think of

keep a mental note and tell Pete when he contacts you. Don't do anything but just carry on as normal. I have a feeling that whatever it is will happen through you, so just keep on your guard and say nothing to anybody. Have I made myself clear?" I am too shocked to speak, I just nod. She stands up and says, "Right then we will leave you to it. Remember just act normally." As she goes to leave I suddenly remember something. "Wait there is something strange that happened." They turn and look at me and I tell them about the customer who thought that Stephen was somebody else. Looking thoughtful his boss says, "Can you remember any names?" Racking my brains I say, "I know that she said his name was Joey but I can't remember his brother's name." Pete smiles and says, "Well if you do just let me know." He hesitates as his boss sweeps out of the room. Turning back he says gently, "I'm sorry Bella. She is a bit full on but doesn't mean anything by it. We are looking out for you just remember that."
I shake my head and watch as they both leave.

Chapter 20

I spend the rest of the day in bed. I can't sleep but need to try and relax. As I lie here all I can think of is the events of the last two days. Nothing makes sense anymore and I can't possibly see how I am connected to anything. Before long I fall into a troubled sleep. It is dark when I wake up and feeling cold I jump out of bed and into the shower. I feel much better when I have finished and pull my dressing gown on feeling a lot warmer. Realising that I haven't eaten since the slice of toast at breakfast I decide to go and get something to eat. I am almost expecting to see Ben's boss and Pete as they appear to have the freedom to come and go as they please. Ben's boss makes me uncomfortable. I don't even know her name which surprises me. Pete is nice though, but I wish that I had the answers to everything that is spinning around in my head.
With annoyance I find that I don't have much in. The only thing that I can make is cheese on toast so I set about making it. I hate being here on my own. The house is lifeless without Ben in it and once again all I wish is for him to return.
There is a sudden loud knock on the door and in surprise

I go to answer it. I am not expecting anybody so look out of the window to see who it is first. I am surprised to see Stephen waiting outside and open the door to see what he wants. As he takes in my appearance a slow smile spreads across his face. "Hi Bella, you look a lot better, although still a tad underdressed."

Blushing I suddenly smell burning and remember the grill. Shouting at him to come in I race back in to the kitchen and quickly pull the grill out. In my haste I drop the melted cheese on my hand and as I feel it burn I drop the grill pan. It makes a terrible sound as it falls to the floor and Stephen races over. Grabbing my hand he marches me over to the sink and runs it under the cold water. Looking at me in amusement he says, "Goodness me Bella. You are a walking disaster. Looking after you must be a full time job." To my surprise he then gently brushes my hair back away from my face. Before I can reply however we hear another voice say, "Yes it is and that job is already taken."

Still holding on to my hand he spins around and there standing in the kitchen is Ben looking extremely tired and disgruntled.

Pulling my hand away I can't get over to him quickly enough. I grab hold of him tightly and squeeze him as hard as I can. "Ben, thank goodness you're home. I've missed you so much." He crushes me to him and buries his face in my hair. Softly he says, "I've missed you too Bella, more than you will ever know."

There is a discreet cough behind us and I remember that Stephen is here. Pulling away I say, "Oh, I'm sorry. Ben this is Stephen De Souza the new store manager at Kinghams. Stephen, this is Ben Hardcastle." Stephen smiles and holds out his hand and Ben looks at him in surprise. They shake hands and Ben says, "I'm sorry but you have me at a disadvantage. Am I missing something. Why are you here and why is Bella in her dressing gown?"

I suddenly see how bad this looks and with a nervous laugh say, "I'm not sure really. I mean I have just had a shower and then Stephen arrived whilst I was making something to eat." Turning towards him I say, "Why did you come Stephen?" Looking a little put out Stephen holds out his hand and I see my phone in it. "I'm sorry Bella but you must have put your phone in my bag by mistake. I thought that you may need it so thought that I would deliver it in person." As I take it I am grateful but surprised that he went to so much trouble. Ben looks at him with his eyes narrowed; I recognise that look and feel the need to interrupt before things get out of hand. "Oh thank you Stephen. You shouldn't have put yourself out. It could have waited until Monday. Would you like a drink, It's the least I can do for all of the help you've given me over last few days?" Stephen smiles thinly saying, "No, I won't hold you both up. I expect that you have a lot of catching up to do. Good to meet you Ben and see you on Monday Bella." They shake hands but you could cut the atmosphere with a knife. Neither looks comfortable with the other and I can't wait for Stephen to leave.

Ben steps forward and says, "I'll show you out Stephen. Thank you for everything. I am sure that Bella will fill me in on all the details." Stephen smiles at me and then I watch as they leave the kitchen.

I set about clearing up the mess and in no time Ben is back. Walking quickly over to me he gathers me in his arms and kisses me with such passion and desperation that it takes my breath away. Pulling back he says huskily, "I have a lot of questions that need answering from you Bella, but they can wait because all I want is you. There has not been a minute since I left that I haven't thought about you." He then sweeps me up and carries me upstairs. Now is not the time for talking. We have more important things to sort out first.

Chapter 21

Ben is back. That is all that I can think of as I lay snuggled up beside him. All that matters is that he is here with me, we can talk later; I just want him as close to me as we can possibly get. He is holding on to me tightly and I wriggle closer to him. Tracing the outline of his face I say, "Don't ever leave me again Ben. I can't take it." Catching hold of my fingers he holds them to his chest. "I'm not going anywhere. This is where I belong, with you." He kisses me gently at first and then with more passion. With excitement I realise that this is going to be a long night.

In fact we don't talk much at all. The night is soon replaced by morning and when I wake up I am overjoyed to find that it was not a dream and Ben really is back. As I open my eyes I see him watching me, his expression soft and loving. Stroking my hair he says, "You are so beautiful Bella. I can't believe how lucky I am." Gently kissing his lips I say, "No Ben, I am the lucky one."

Once again we don't do much talking and all we really want is to be together. However soon hunger takes over and we decide to go out for lunch due to the fact that I

haven't got any food in the house.
As we get ready we talk about general things, both of us skirting the issues that we really want to talk about.
By the time we are sitting in the pub waiting for our food we realise that things need to be said. As we sit together holding hands Ben says, "Tell me about Stephen Bella, when did he arrive?" Looking at him in surprise I say, "The day after you left. He is Simon's replacement." Looking thoughtful Ben says, "That is what puzzles me. I didn't appoint a replacement. So the question is if I didn't then who did?" I look at him in shock. He then adds, "It would also appear that you two have become quite good friends in my absence. How has that come about?" He is looking at me with a hard expression and I suddenly feel angry. Snatching my hand away I say, "Well for your information we are not good friends just colleagues. You are a fine one to talk though, from what I've heard you've rekindled one of your old flames whilst you've been gone." Looking at me in surprise he grabs back hold of my hand. Leaning towards me he fixes me with an intense look. "Well for your information Bella, nothing was re kindled with anyone. I have been working very hard to solve a problem that doesn't appear to exist. I may have spent time with a friend but that is all she is and as she was the one who asked for my help in the first place it is not that much of

a surprise." He then strokes my mouth and then kisses it gently. Pulling away he says, "You have nothing to worry about. My heart is yours Bella, it always has been." Looking down I say, "Then why do I feel so worried Ben?" Our food arrives and interrupts our conversation. We eat in silence both wrapped up in our own thoughts.

As soon as I have finished Ben says, "Come on, let's get out of here. I'm taking you home and we will talk. You can ask me anything. I am not having you feeling like this Bella, especially as there is no reason to."

I follow him in surprise, suddenly worried at what I may find out.

As soon as we get home Ben makes us some drinks and we curl up by the fire. Holding me against him he says, "Right now ask away." Suddenly I feel awkward. I am not sure where to begin so I just say, "I would like to know if I am just a job to you." Ben looks amazed and laughs in surprise. "Of course you are not a job to me. What ever gives you that idea?" Shrugging I say miserably, "I overheard some girls talking last night at the hotel bar. They were talking about you and Vanessa and said that you had been apart because of some job that you were sorting out and that now that you were back the two of you were making up for lost time, which is why you didn't go to the awards evening. You also told Stephen that it was your job to look after me." As I say the words I choke back the tears. How I felt is flooding back to me and I still can't believe that those girls were setting me up. Ben is looking at me in disbelief and I add, "It's also a bit of a coincidence that you have turned up now after your boss told me that they thought that I was connected to something happening at the moment. You may have been sent back to find out what it is." Now Ben is looking incredulous and suddenly extremely angry. "Rewind Bella. What on earth is going on? Firstly what's this about the awards ceremony and why has my boss contacted you? I think that you had better start at the beginning."

Looking at him in surprise I can see that he has no idea of what has been going on. I fill him in on the events of the last two days and by the end of it his face is set in stone. Looking at me incredulously he says, "I came back because I missed you Bella. I didn't know any of this. I told Vanessa that I would be coming home and would help her from here. There has been no conversation with my boss or Pete, but I can assure you now that there soon will be. Your friend Stephen has also got some explaining to do. I am so angry." He gets up and starts pacing up and down. I can see his mind working and I feel more confused now than I did before. If Ben wasn't told then why not? None of it makes

sense. I feel reassured about his relationship with Vanessa but I still can't work out their connection. This however is definitely not the time to ask him about it. He is on the warpath now, that much is evident. He carries on ranting getting more and more irate as he goes.
"So you are telling me that you spent the night in a hotel room with someone who gave you drugs and alcohol and got you in a terrible state after hearing lies at the hotel bar?" Nervously I say, "I don't think that it was Stephen's fault. He was quite kind to me and helped me. It was also him who saved me at the gym." Spinning around Ben almost shouts, "What happened at the gym?" Telling him the story his eyes darken until they are almost black and flash dangerously. His voice suddenly changes and becomes low and menacing. "A real knight in shining armour then. Hmm, I wonder."
In shock I say, "You don't seriously think that Stephen had anything to do with any of this. Like I said, he just happened to be around when I needed help. You should be thanking him." His eyes flashing Ben says, "Oh don't worry Bella, I fully intend on finding out exactly why he helped you."
I can't help but feel a bit sorry for Stephen. Despite his arrogant ways I have found him to be quite kind really and I couldn't have got through the past few days without his help. Ben however does not appear to share

my gratitude and is still pacing up and down looking angrier than I have ever seen him. Standing up I go over to him and grabbing hold of his hands look him firmly in the eye. "One thing your boss said to me applies now." He looks at me in surprise and I say, "She told me to lose the emotion and look at the facts. If we do that things may become clearer." Suddenly Ben's face relaxes and his mouth twitches. "So you are in training to become an operative now are you?" Pushing him away I say in mock indignation, "Don't you think I could be?" Laughing he says, "Over my dead body Bella. There is no way on God's earth that I would allow you to tread that particular path. It's not a life that I would wish on anyone, especially you."

"But it's ok for you." I say sadly, wondering again what he has had to do in the past. Coming up to me Ben holds me tightly. Looking gently at me he says, "I can't change my past Bella, but I can have a say in my future. I will walk away from that part of me as soon as I can. There will be no new operations and all I want is for us to be together, building our future together."

As I hug him back I take comfort from the fact that he is here. Things may not be ideal and I know that there will be fireworks to come, but as long as we have each other we can get through it. That much I do know.

Chapter 22

Ben wakes up early the next day. We are back to work and he is on a mission.
I watch him as he gets ready. "What are you going to do?" I ask, wondering what his plan is. His face is set in a grim determination and he says, "I am going to get the answers that I need. I won't stop until I know what's going on."
Coming over he sits on the bed and pulls me up towards him. "I love you Bella, never forget that." He kisses me and my insides melt with love for him." Pulling reluctantly away he says, "Listen, you just carry on as normal. I'll call you later and let you know what's going on. We can eat out again if you like to save you worrying about doing any shopping." I just nod but resolve to get some supplies in. What I want the most is to spend our evening in, just the two of us. I don't want to share him with anyone just yet.
I wonder what the day will bring. Life is certainly not dull at the moment and all I actually want is for things to settle down and get back to normal.
April is already in when I arrive and smiles saying, "Good weekend?" Laughing to myself I think, if only she knew. Nodding I say happily, "Ben's home at last."

She smiles broadly saying, "Thank goodness for that. I can tell that you have missed him. Let's hope he doesn't have to go away for a while." I nod in agreement and then turn the computer on to catch up with my emails. With a sinking feeling I see one from Stephen scheduling our meeting. What with everything that has gone on I completely forgot about it. It is for 12.30pm so I don't have much time to come up with the five suggestions that he needs. Turning to April I ask for her help. Two heads are better than one as they say and we spend the next hour trying to come up with some feasible ideas.

I have a meeting with a Rep before I have to see him which helps to take my mind off the coming confrontation.

Alison is one of my favourite Reps and I have known her for years. She sells me a prestige range of cookware and I am interested in the new ranges that she has. As if the God's are smiling on me she excitedly tells me of her companies plans to launch a new exciting brand. They are offering various promotions to their good customers which I pounce on eagerly. There will be a television and marketing campaign that will launch the brand and they will provide promotional offers and material to help with an in-store promotion. Happily I sign up to it, grateful that I will have something concrete to discuss at my dreaded meeting.

Soon the hour approaches and April waves me off sympathetically. As I reach Stephen's office I see Emily, the Cosmetics buyer exiting his office. On seeing me she pulls a face saying in a whisper, "Good luck Bella. He is in a worse mood than usual. God help you if you're unprepared." Thanking her I head off towards the office with a sinking feeling.

I knock on the door and hear a brusque, "Come in." Pushing the door open I see Stephen sitting at the desk. He just looks up and gestures towards the seat in front of his desk. Once I have sat down he raises his eyes and his blue eyes stare at me with a hard expression. "Good afternoon Bella, I hope that you have recovered from your many ordeals." As he says it his face relaxes and a broad grin breaks out over his face. Blushing I reply, "Yes thank you." Coughing nervously I say, "Oh and I must thank you for all of your help. You were so kind and I really appreciated it." He leans back and still staring at me smiles gently. "It was my pleasure. You bring out the protector in me which surprises me." He then leans forward holding my eyes with his and says softly. "It's a rare quality that you have Bella. I have only ever seen it in one other person before and it intrigues me. You are so vulnerable, it brings out a side to me that I never knew existed. I am not surprised that

Ben snapped you up so quickly." Blushing I don't know what to say and just look at him in embarrassment. He puts me out of my misery by looking down at my report and says briskly, "Right then let's see how we can improve things in homewares."
The next hour is spent going over everything in the report. I tell him of the ideas that April and I have come up with and then finish off with the new promotion. By the end of it he looks suitably impressed saying, "Good work Bella. I can see that you have given it a lot of thought, unlike some that I have seen. We will start implementing some of these straight away and you never know you may win the competition." Looking at him in surprise I say, "What competition?" Stephen smiles wickedly saying, "I thought that I would introduce an incentive, so for the department that brings in the biggest increase over a 3 month period I am offering a prize." Looking interested I say, "What is it?" Laughing he says, "I haven't decided yet but I am sure that I will come up with something to get your competitive spirit going." He then looks at his watch and says, "Right then I think we've finished here. How about taking lunch with me? I for one am hungry and could do with some stimulating company for a change." I look at him in surprise, my heart sinking. This isn't good and I know that Ben wouldn't like it. I can't think of an excuse quickly

enough and standing up he holds out his hand to me. "Come on, I know a great little deli not for from here and it will give me the opportunity to make sure that you don't get into any more trouble, for the next hour at least." He obviously finds his words amusing and I have no other option than to follow him.

Chapter 23

Stephen takes me to a local deli. With a sinking feeling I realise that it is the same one that I used to come to with Nathan. I haven't come here since the day he accosted me outside and it brings me nothing but unhappy memories.
We purchase our lunch and Stephen leads me over to a secluded table in the corner. Winking at me he says, "Away from prying eyes. We don't want anybody seeing us and getting the wrong idea do we?" Once again I blush and he laughs enjoying my obvious discomfort.
I decide to try and find out more about him. However he dodges all of my questions about his past and personal life and his answers give nothing away. Feeling frustrated I say, "You don't give much away do you Stephen?" He stares at me which is strangely compelling and says, "I am a very private person Bella. I find it difficult to talk about myself, which is probably why I don't have anyone special to share my life with. I am much more interested in talking about you." Returning his gaze I say, "You should open up more Stephen. Underneath I can tell that you are a kind and considerate person with a lot to give. You should relax more and

then maybe you will meet someone special." Still looking directly at me he says, "I always want what I can't have. Although I am a great believer that if you work hard enough at getting what you want you will be rewarded in the end."

Pushing his lunch away he says, "Anyway we should get back. Thanks for the company Bella, as always I have enjoyed it. Maybe we could do it again tomorrow." I am not sure what to say and just smile. Laughing he waves me through in front of him and then follows me out on to the pavement. As we walk back to the store he says, "Are you planning on going to the gym at all this week? If you are I could help work out a proper programme for you." Laughing I say, "My days at the gym are well and truly over for now. After the last time I am sticking to a gentler form of fitness." Smiling he says, "That's a shame. I was quite looking forward to seeing what trouble you would get into next." By the time we have reached the store I am no further forward knowing anything about him than I was before.

Luckily the rest of the day passes by as normal and after stopping for supplies on the way home I get home to find the house empty.

I start preparing dinner and it's not long before I hear the front door slam. Looking up I see Ben coming into the kitchen and he doesn't look happy. Raising my eyes up I say, "Bad Day?" Looking angrily at me he says, "You could say that Bella." I suddenly feel uncomfortable as he looks meaningfully at me. "What about your day Bella. Anything to tell me?" Suddenly I know where this is going which explains his bad mood. "If you are referring to my lunch buddy then what do you want to know?" Looking exasperated Ben comes over and pulls me to him. "I thought that I told you to keep away from him Bella. There's something I don't like about him and he is targeting you for some reason." Pushing him away I say, "That is easier said than done Ben. He is still my boss and I couldn't think of a quick enough excuse to get out of having lunch with him. Oh and for your information I thought that I may find out something about him that I could tell you about." Looking thoughtful Ben says, "And did you?" Lowering my eyes I say, "No. He is impossible to read. He was more interested in me." Sighing Ben says, "I bet he was." As I look at him a sudden thought comes into my mind. "Ben, if you are so unhappy with this situation, why don't you do something about it?" Ben grabs a bottle of wine from the store and as he pours us a glass he says, "I only wish that I could. I am afraid this is out of my hands. We are stuck with him, at least for the short term." His reply surprises me. "But you own the store. Surely what you say goes." Shaking his head he says, "Not this time

Bella. We have to let matters take their course. It doesn't mean that I am happy about it though." Handing me the glass he says, "But one thing I can control and that is his obvious interest in you. Please keep away from him Bella. I don't want you to be drawn into whatever this is, so promise me you will do as I ask."

As I take a gulp of wine I feel unsettled. Ben isn't telling me everything and once again I feel like a pawn in someone else's game. He goes off to get changed and I carry on making the dinner. When he comes back he sets about helping me and I notice that he is distracted. Something is on his mind that he hasn't told me and I resolve to get it out of him.

After we have eaten and cleared away Ben says, "Do you mind if I spend an hour in my study Bella? I'm sorry to ask but there is something that needs doing." Feeling cross I say, "Ok, but then will you do something for me?" His eyes light up and mischievously he says, "There is a lot that I want to do for you Bella, just say the word." Raising my eyes up I fix him with a hard stare and say, "Not that, well not at first anyway, but will you tell me what you found out today?" This obviously surprises him as I normally never question him and with a sigh he says, "I'll try Bella. It's not as easy as you think though." I reply shortly, "Well try then. I am fed up of always being kept in the dark, especially about matters that concern me."

He heads off to his study and I resolve not to let him get away with it. We are in this together and he owes me an explanation at the very least.

The hour soon goes and tentatively I knock on his study door. Taking him in a coffee I notice how tired he looks. Handing it to him I pull a chair up and sit down opposite. I need to see his face when he tells me whatever it is he has to say. I mean business and I want him to see that. Ruefully he says, "So the time for explanations is upon us." Nodding I say, "It's not too much to ask is it?" Sipping his coffee he looks at me as though searching for something and then his expression changes to one of defeat. "Ok Bella, I will tell you but I warn you, you won't like what you hear."

Suddenly I feel afraid. Whatever is he going to tell me?

Chapter 24

Ben looks carefully at me as he begins. "As you know, before I met you I had not long finished a very demanding job. It was around the time of the banking crisis which if you believed the rumours concerned me more than most. Many people thought that I had a hand in it and hated me for what I had to do. In fact the truth is very different. My organisation was alerted to the problems in the banking industry several months before the collapse. I, with other colleagues, were sent in to try and limit the damage. I was given the job at Montague's. Claude Montague was a despicable human being who ran the well respected bank into the ground. He appointed his friends to senior positions who were in no way qualified for the jobs they did. He made several dodgy deals and invested the bank's money in schemes that were doomed to fail from the start. They were losing money fast and it was my job to sort it all out." I listen to him riveted to what he is telling me. I always knew that he had had a difficult time there and many people had hated him. I expect that is why I never questioned him about it before. It is obviously a time in his life that he would rather forget. I notice his expression change to one of anger as he carries on.

"Not only was Claude a terrible businessman but he was also a vile husband to his wife Vanessa. I had heard the rumours of his affairs and her fragile mental state and like everyone else just dismissed it." Suddenly his face softens and he says, "It was at a particularly boring banking dinner that I met Vanessa for the first time. We were sat next to each other and she was nothing like I had imagined. She was small and vulnerable and very nervous. It took some doing but I managed to draw her out a little and discovered that she was actually very intelligent and highly amusing." As he talks about Vanessa, I start to feel a bit uncomfortable. Do I really want to hear about this after all?

Carrying on he says, "It was obvious that Claude had brought along his mistress to the event. I had heard the rumours and noticed that he spent a lot of time with another woman. Everybody saw him blatantly flirting with her and it soon became obvious that they were together. I stuck close to Vanessa out of pity at first and then because I was really enjoying her company." Suddenly he looks at me with concern saying, "You may not like what I say next Bella but you must understand what things were like for me at the time. I was doing a job that I hated with people that hated me. It was extremely lonely and there was nobody in my life at all

except work. Spending time with Vanessa I realised how much we needed each other. She was lost too and we took comfort in each other. We started an affair that night which I will not apologise for. When I first met her she was broken. I watched over the coming weeks and months her blossom into a confident, funny, beautiful woman." My eyes fill up with tears. Not for the reason that Ben must think but because of what he told me. I actually couldn't love him anymore than I do at this moment. Leaning over towards him I take his hands in mine. "It's ok Ben. I understand, carry on."
Looking slightly relieved he continues. "Well soon everybody began to see what I saw. Vanessa began to build a life for herself out of her husband's shadow. She started to mix with others and was considered good company. She had emerged as a great beauty and with her new found confidence she was amazing. The trouble is though her husband also started to see her in a new light. He started paying more attention to her which irritated her at first and then worried her. He demanded more of her time and when she resisted he grew violent." Listening with horror, I picture poor Vanessa and suddenly know what Ben is going to say next. A pained expression comes over his face as he says, "I hadn't heard from her for a few days and I was worried. She normally rang me several times a day and hadn't turned

up to our last date. I was extremely worried and took some papers around to their house in the pretence that I needed them signed. What I found will live with me forever. Claude had badly attacked her. She was beaten black and blue and he had raped her. She was a total mess and I urged her to come away with me." Tears are now running down my face at the thought of poor Vanessa and what she went through. Even though I don't know her the sight of Ben telling me what happened makes me realise just how devastating it was. Ben lowers his eyes and says, "She wouldn't come with me. I offered to help her in any way that I could. I wanted to find him and beat him as he had her but she wouldn't let me. She begged me to let her deal with it herself. She wouldn't even let me call her a doctor but I couldn't just leave her. I arranged for the doctor that we use through the organisation to come and see to her. I assured her that no questions would be asked and nobody would know. I then told her that if she wouldn't let me confront him then I would make sure that we had enough evidence on him to ruin him. By the time I had finished with him he would be publicly ridiculed and would never work in the City again.
I had never been so angry in my life before and despite the job that I had to do gathered enough evidence against him to bury him."

He breaks off and says, "Are you ok Bella? This is difficult for me dredging it all up again but it must be equally difficult to hear." Shaking my head I say, "No, I'm fine. Please carry on I want to know everything." Looking worried he says, "However as it turned out I didn't need any of it. Early one morning I took a call from Vanessa. She was hysterical and said that Claude had committed suicide. I raced around to their house and she hadn't called the police or anyone. He was lying face down on the desk in the Study and was as she said dead. Quickly I called the Police and an Ambulance. I tried to comfort her as she was in shock. I stayed with her and guided her through. Despite the fact that she hated him he was still her husband and there were endless questions and procedures to follow. With him dead the bank was in crisis. I filled in for him until they could find someone to take over his position. As it was they found a well respected banker to succeed him who greatly turned their fortunes around. Shortly after I left Montague's for good."

As I look at him I still get the feeling that he is holding something back from me. I know him inside and out and recognise that there is more to this story than he is telling me. He stopped looking at me towards the end and kept his eyes lowered. I also noticed a faint flush on his face, but decide not to press the matter.

Looking at me with concern he says softly, "This now brings me to the part that you are not going to like." I look up in surprise. It's bad enough hearing about his relationship with Vanessa. I thought that was what he meant, suddenly I feel afraid. "My work was over at the bank and it had left me emotionally scarred. Vanessa was picking up the pieces of her life and I realised that she needed space and time to get used to life without Claude. Before I left however she came to see me. She was grateful for everything that I had done for her and wanted to help me in return. I had told her once about my wish to buy my own department store and so she offered to help me. She would put the money up for me to invest in a family run department store. She knew the owners and they wanted to retire. The market was crashing so she knew that we would get a good price. I was to run the store and she would be my financial backer. As she was now the owner of a soon to be successful bank, money would be no object. The bank would back me financially and have an equal share of ownership." Looking at me with concern he says, "So as you can see, I am not in this on my own. Vanessa and the bank are tied to me and I have to answer to them. This is why I owe them my loyalty. When she called and asked me for my help I had no other option but to go."
I feel confused. "What was the problem that you had to

go and fix Ben and why couldn't you come home at all. I thought it was part of your job with the organisation?" Looking worried he says, "When Vanessa contacted me she said that she had problems at the bank. She suspected that somebody was siphoning money off and had no way of finding out. She wanted my help and needed me to once again take up a position in the bank. When I ran it through my boss she said that they had not noticed any strange activity and was surprised at the request. They had been keeping a close eye on all of the banks since the crisis and hadn't noticed anything untoward. She came back to me later and said that after some investigations she wanted me to do as Vanessa said because she thought that there was more to it than Vanessa was telling me. I was to do what Vanessa said and report back anything strange. I stayed at the flat that we use in the City and it soon became apparent that things were not that straightforward. Vanessa insisted that I accompany her to various functions, saying that I would be helping her as somebody was stalking her. She didn't feel safe and wanted me to protect her. I found nothing untoward at the bank and despite looking at everything with a fine tooth comb came up empty handed. It soon became apparent that the reason I was there was to stay close to her." Seeing my expression change he says reassuringly. "Nothing happened between us. She knew that I was with you and respected that. However she wanted to be seen with me to get a message to whoever was targeting her that she was protected. However as the weeks went on I began to have my doubts. I hadn't heard from my boss at all and there was nothing to suggest that Vanessa was in any danger. So I told her that I would be coming home and to contact me if she needed to night or day. She wasn't happy about it and begged for me to stay but as you know I couldn't stay away a minute more than I had to." As he speaks I feel even more confused. "But what does all of this have to do with the stores and Stephen?" Grimly Ben says, "It appears that whilst I was away, chasing something that wasn't there, a lot was unfolding in my absence. Pete had got word that the stores were losing money and the bank was concerned. They were putting in somebody to try and discover what was happening and that person is Stephen." Looking at Ben in shock I say, "But why didn't they tell you, surely you should have been informed." Looking angry Ben says, "Apparently when Pete told my boss she told him to keep it from me. They needed to look into it first as she thought that there was more to it than they were being led to believe. So that is where we are now. Stephen is apparently trying to look for where the hole is financially on the instructions of the bank, who own half of the business. I am to let him do his job and not to interfere in any way."

Still worried I get up and go over to Ben. Sitting on his lap I bury my face into his chest. "I am sorry Ben. You must be worried. The fact that it was all kept from you is awful. Hopefully he will find out where the money is going and we can return to normal." Ben strokes my hair but is silent. I know that he wont like being in control and in my heart I feel that all of this is just the start of something.

Chapter 25

Ben and I decided to spend the rest of the evening just watching TV and trying to switch off from the problems at the store. He was very quiet though and I know that something is troubling him. Thinking about Stephen I wonder what he will find. I am surprised that he is at Kinghams though; I would have thought that he would be better placed at head office to do his digging.

The next day, Ben goes off to head office and I make my way to Kinghams. I have a lot to do this week as I need to organise the sale so get in early with a view to getting started.

As I walk to my office I hear somebody calling my name. Turning around I see Stephen racing up behind me. "Bella, wait up," he says and with a sinking feeling I do as he says. Ben has urged me to keep away from him and I wonder just how easy this is going to be. As he reaches me he smiles saying, "You're in bright and early, any reason?" Smiling back I say, "I just want to get a head start on planning the sale. There's a lot to do and I find that I can get a lot done before the phones start ringing and distracting me." Laughing he nods in agreement. "You're right there. Anyway, I have to go to head office today and I was wondering if you would accompany me." I look at him in surprise. "Oh, I'm sorry to ask Stephen but is it urgent; it's just that I have so much to do here?" I feel flustered. Ben would hit the roof if I turned up with Stephen. Looking thoughtful he says, "Actually it is. I have set up a meeting for you with their homewares buyer Susan. She has been doing really well there and has come up with some good suggestions. I thought that you could swap ideas and put your heads together. You also have some good ideas that I think that she would benefit from. I know that you are busy but think that it would be worth the time spent. It's not until lunch time so you can make a start here and then when we come back I can help you catch up if you want." Not knowing what to say I just nod and say, "Where shall I meet you?" I notice a small triumphant smile flash across his face and he says, "12.30pm by the staff entrance. The meeting is at 1.30pm so we should have plenty of time to get there." Smiling at him I nod and then quickly head off to my office.

When I get there I decide to phone Ben. I had better tell him as it would be awkward if he saw me turning up with Stephen. He answers quickly, "Hi Bella. Is everything ok?" Nervously I say, "Yes its fine. I just thought that I would let you know that Stephen has arranged a meeting with me and Susan at 1.30pm and we will be coming over to head office." I hear him sigh and he says irritably, "Oh has he now. Well I don't like the idea of you two having a cosy drive over here and then back again." In surprise I say, "He told me that he has a meeting there too. Did you know?" "Yes but I didn't expect him to bring you with him. Just watch him Bella and let me know if he says anything. I'll see you when you get here." He puts the phone down and I can tell that he is annoyed. I knew that he would be but it can't be helped. I am sure that he is wrong about Stephen. Why on earth would he be interested in me?

The dreaded hour soon comes and I find myself walking next to Stephen towards his car. As I get into the passenger seat I notice that it is well looked after and in pristine condition. There is not a speck of dust inside and nothing is out of place. It is almost as if it has just been delivered. Looking at him as he takes his seat behind the wheel I say, "This is a nice car Stephen. You must have it valeted; it is so clean and tidy." He laughs saying, "I am afraid that is my OCD coming out. I like everything in its place and get extremely irate if it isn't. I'm like it at home too. It's probably best that I do live alone, I would be a nightmare to live with." I laugh glad that I have found something out about him, inconsequential as it is.

As we drive he puts some music on low. It is a classical

track that is haunting. In surprise I say, "I wouldn't have had you down as a classical music lover either." Laughing he says, "What did you have me down as." Blushing I say, "I thought that you would be more into Rock music." Smiling wickedly at me he says, "Oh I'm into a lot of things Bella. I can try my hand at most things." Shifting uncomfortably in my seat I look out of the window. Interrupting my thoughts he says, "It must be nice to have Ben home." In surprise I say, "Yes it is. I missed him when he was away." Looking thoughtful he says, "Does he go away a lot?" Feeling uncomfortable talking about Ben I just say, "No, thankfully." Then he says softly, "If I was him I wouldn't go away at all without you. Despite the fact that you are obviously accident prone, I wouldn't trust anyone around you." Startled I say, "Why do you say that?" "Well you probably don't realise it Bella but you are a very attractive woman with a vulnerability that makes men want to protect you. It is a deadly combination that makes people do things that they know they shouldn't." Now I feel extremely uncomfortable. I don't know how to react or what to say so I say nothing and can feel my face flushing. Suddenly he laughs and says, "I am embarrassing you. I am sorry about that. Forget that I said it. It was inappropriate and I apologise."
For a little while we just listen to the music and then I

say, "Tell me about yourself Stephen. How did you get to where you are today?" I can tell that I have surprised him with my question and he merely says, "Oh it's no big secret. I just worked my way up through various positions and took advantage of any promotions that came my way. Throw in a little bit of luck and hey presto here I am." I smile but realise that he hasn't told me anything at all. He is certainly a master of avoidance. By the time we reach head office I am no closer to knowing anything about him.

Stephen and I sign in and I am directed to the homewares buying office to meet Susan. Before Stephen goes to his meeting he says, "I'll meet you back here Bella. It will probably take an hour. If it's going to be longer I'll let you know." As I head towards my meeting I hope that it all goes smoothly. I don't want any more drama at the moment. It's taken me a while to get my head around what Ben told me last night.

I had a good meeting with Susan, who I have met before. Stephen was right she does have some good ideas and we chatted happily about our departments. The hour flew past and after saying my goodbyes I headed back to the staff entrance to meet Stephen. As I walked through the store I heard someone calling my name. "Bella, wait a minute." Spinning around I see Ben racing towards me. I have to remember where I am and resist the urge to run over to him. Smiling as he approaches I say, "This is a nice surprise." He grins and says, "I'm glad I caught you. I got stuck in a meeting and thought that you may have gone already. Have you had lunch yet?" Shaking my head I say, "No, but I have to meet Stephen now and head back to Kinghams. I'll probably just grab a sandwich from the Canteen when I get back." Shaking his head he says, "No need, I'll take you to lunch and then drop you back. I have to go over there this afternoon anyway." Before I can answer I see Stephen approaching us looking a bit annoyed. He looks at Ben warily and then holding out his hand says, "Good to see you again Mr Hardcastle." I watch as they shake hands and feel exasperated at the tension that is suddenly in the air. Ben replies, "You too Stephen. I hope that you are finding everything you need. If not please come straight to me." Stephen smiles and then says, "Are you ready Bella?" Feeling awkward I look between them and Ben says, "I'll drop Bella back Stephen. I'm coming over to the store this afternoon and I thought that I would treat her to some lunch first." Stephen nods but I can tell that he is annoyed. His eyes flashing he turns to me and says, "I'll see you later then. I haven't forgotten my promise to help you this afternoon." With a sinking feeling I see Ben's eyes narrow and quickly nod at Stephen and pull Ben away. As we go Ben whispers angrily, "What was that all about. What is he helping you with?" Suddenly I feel exhausted. I only want to get on with my work and feel as if I am being pulled one way and then another by the two of them. Raising my eyes up I say, "Oh it's nothing. I tried to get out of coming and said that I had a lot on. His response was that he would help me with it when we got back." Ben looks tense and not at all happy. I just wish that things would be resolved soon as all of this animosity is bringing me down.

Chapter 26

Ben and I have a nice lunch on the way back to Kinghams. I have a sneaky feeling that there is no reason for him to come to the store and it was just an excuse to keep me away from Stephen.
As soon as we arrive back he says, "I'll take you home Bella. We can leave your car here tonight." Looking at him I say, "Then how will I get here tomorrow?" With a triumphant look Ben says, "I will bring you in. I didn't tell you before but I am moving in for a while. It is about time I spent more time here and this seems like a good time to sort things out here." I just look at him with a blank expression. He looks very pleased with himself but I can see right through him. It has nothing at all to do with the store, that much I know. It's just his way of keeping an eye on Stephen, just in case he tries to get closer to me. Winking at me he heads off to his office and wearily I return to mine.
I throw myself into my work to try and forget about the two of them for a while. April helps me and we soon have the Sale organised. Half way through there is a knock on the door and Stephen comes into the office. April looks uncomfortable and I look up with a sinking

feeling. "Hello Bella, April, I've come to offer my services to you both." April looks at him open mouthed and I am surprised as I never even thought for a minute that he would really help out. Shaking my head I smile saying, "Thanks Stephen but there is really no need. April and I have it covered but thanks for your offer." Coming over he sits down on to a nearby chair and looks at us both. "Good, you must have both worked really hard to get it done." Turning to me he says, "How was your meeting with Susan Bella, I never did get a chance to discuss it with you?" I smile and say, "Good actually. You were right she has some good ideas which I will definitely use here." Looking thoughtful he says, "Well if you've now got the time maybe you would like to come for a coffee and we could discuss them. You too April, it's the least I could do for you both after all of your hard work." Looking at April I think that she is about to expire. He flashes her a warm grin and I see the colour rise in her cheeks. Catching his eye I grin at him and say, "Great, come on April, we could do with a shot of caffeine after this lot."

Over coffee we chat about the department and our plans to improve it. Stephen is at his most charming and it amuses me to see the effect he has on April. Laughing to myself I notice that Stephen has a way with the ladies. He could be quite dangerous really and I am sure that he

could have his pick of partners if he chose to. I catch him staring at me a couple of times but I pretend not to notice. Even if he does have designs on me I am not interested. I couldn't love anyone more than I do Ben and he really does have nothing to worry about, despite the fact that he obviously thinks that he does.
After coffee we return to our relevant offices and April fans herself as we sit down. "Oh my God. If I wasn't already in a relationship I could so go there." Laughing I raise my eyes up saying, "I thought you hated him April, you've soon changed your tune." Grinning she says sardonically, "I wonder why?" Laughing we both get on with our work.

Later on that evening I remember to ask Ben if he has heard anything from his boss about the situation. Looking grim he nods and my heart does a somersault. "Yes it would appear that the stores are indeed losing money. We can't find out the source but Pete is working on it at the moment. We are not sure for how long it has been going on but it could have cost us thousands of pounds already."
Shocked I can't believe what I am hearing. "Is it serious, I mean could it ruin the stores?" Sighing heavily Ben says, "If left undiscovered, yes of course. The sooner we find out where the money is going and who is

responsible the better it will be." As I digest his words I say, "Did they find out anything on Stephen?" Ben's eyes narrow and he says irritably, "No, apparently he is who he says he is and his work history is impressive. There is nothing to suggest that he could be anything other than who he says he is. The bank trusts him and is impressed with his work so far. My boss is still unconvinced though and has resolved to keep on digging."
Noticing my worried expression Ben smiles and pulls me up. "Enough about work Bella. I still haven't made up for all those weeks that I was away. Seeing you today at head office was like a breath of fresh air in an otherwise extremely stressful day. It made me realise just how lucky I am to have found you again. I am going to look forward to spending more time with you over the coming weeks. Right now though all I want is an early night with the woman I love." Leaning down he tilts my face towards his and kisses me gently at first and then with more urgency. I feel the excitement growing in me as he crushes me towards him, running his hand over my back and shifting so that I am firmly against him. Breaking away I can see the longing in his eyes and I run my fingers through his hair and then pull him towards me. I don't think that I will ever get enough of him. Just one look is all it takes. Whatever the future may bring it

doesn't matter as long as I am with him.

Chapter 27

The week has passed by uneventfully thank goodness. Stephen has kept his distance and I am enjoying having Ben near me at the store. We go to lunch most days and have settled into quite a routine already. I am actually dreading him returning to head office and have got used to him nearby.
I am excited because tonight Ben and I have been invited to Boris's birthday party. It's not as much as a party but dinner at their house with just a few other couples. What with the dramas lately it will be good to catch up with our good friends for some light relief.
As soon as we arrive we are surrounded by familiar faces. I am happy to see Camilla and her husband Henry. Camilla is Boris's mad cousin and a typical Sloane ranger. "Bella, my darling, it's been far too long," she cries kissing me three times on the cheek. "And darling Ben, come here you gorgeous creature." I laugh as she grabs Ben and kisses him a lot more than three times. Raising his eyes up at me I can't help but giggle. She has always coveted Ben, it doesn't matter that her husband is next to her, she wouldn't care. Phoebe grabs my hand and pulls me over to Boris. "Happy Birthday Boris," I say giving him a warm hug. Then I give him his gift

which he is embarrassed to receive. Boris doesn't like a fuss made of him and Phoebe grins at me as we enjoy his discomfort.

We soon settle in for the evening. As well as the six of us there are also two other couples who we know by sight but not to talk to. Samantha and Mark are Phoebe's next door neighbours who I know that Phoebe adores as she has spoken about them often enough. The other couple, Martin and Angela are from Boris's work. They work at the Bank with him and met whilst they were there.

Phoebe has cooked a fabulous meal and we all enjoy chatting at her huge table. I always feel so at home at their house. They are like family to me and I know that Ben adores them as much as I do. After we have heard all of their gossip I hear Boris ask Ben about his time at the bank. I can see that Ben is uncomfortable as they don't know about his other life and he won't want to lie to them.

With half an ear on their conversation I am suddenly aware that Phoebe is talking to me. "Tell me about your new boss Bella. I've heard that he is quite a catch." Surprised I say, "How do you know that?" Phoebe winks and says, my friend Amanda went in the other day and apparently he walked past and the assistant almost swooned. Amanda asked who he was and the assistant told her. She said that she had never seen such a hottie. Her words not mine." Phoebe grins and Camilla pipes up, "Oh my God, I must come and shop there soon. I know I will meet you for lunch Bella and you could introduce us." We laugh and I notice that the men have listened to every word. Boris and Henry look amused but Ben looks annoyed. Seeing his expression Phoebe whispers to me, "What's with Ben, doesn't he like his new manager." Pulling a face I say quietly, "That's an understatement, he's gone all alpha male on me and I feel as if I am working in a Testosterone pressure cooker that will explode any minute." Phoebe laughs gleefully. "You are so lucky Bella. What I wouldn't give for that working environment. Robert Grundy is no comparison." I laugh thinking of Phoebe's boss at the Art Gallery. He must be at least 65, with a comb over and a distinct paunch. Camilla won't let up and says, "What's his name, do we know him?" Ben says, "Stephen De Souza." Frowning Camilla says, "That name rings a bell with me. It's so distinctive which is probably why. What about you Henry, does it ring any bells with you?" Henry looks thoughtful and says, "It does actually. It can't be the same guy though because the one I am thinking of is away on a world cruise at the moment, and he is certainly no sex God, as Camilla would put it." Quickly I look at Ben who suddenly looks very interested. He pulls out his phone and I see him quickly send a text. The others carry on talking about world cruises and I say to him quietly, "What are you thinking?" "I don't know, just a hunch. We'll know soon for certain." He doesn't elaborate and I am drawn back into the conversation.

About ten minutes later I notice a text come through for Ben and holding out his phone to Camilla he says, "Is this him?" Grabbing the phone she looks at the photo that Ben was sent and screws her face up in surprise. "Definitely not. If this was him I wouldn't be with Henry that much I will say." Henry laughs good naturedly and also looks at the photo. "No, that's not him. Way too good looking and much younger." Camilla still looks confused and says, "I have seen him before though. I can't think where but I wouldn't forget that face in a hurry. Oh it's going to annoy me all night now." I can see that Ben is very interested and I wonder if Camilla will be able to shed some light on who she thinks he is. We carry on and have coffee and brandy in the living room. As we sit around chatting Camilla suddenly jumps up shouting, "Got it! Boris, take me to your computer at once." Boris jumps up and they go into his study. Ben and I follow them and Camilla says, "It may take me some time and may not even be him but I think that he was seeing Veronica Ashworthy." Henry ambles in and turning to him she says, "Don't you remember the scandal Henry. He nods and turning to us she says, "Well, Veronica came home one afternoon and found her husband Ralph in bed with his secretary. Apparently they had been having an affair and she was devastated. She threw him out of the house and things got very messy. One night though she turns up at a charity event with the most drop dead gorgeous guy on her arm. She was positively glowing and looked ten years younger. Ralph looked like he was going to have a heart attack. I mean she was radiant, and there were no prizes for knowing why, given the fact that they couldn't keep their hands off each other all night."

I share a look with Ben and we are riveted by the story. Frantically Camilla taps away on the computer as she carries on telling us. "Well Ralph got jealous and Veronica got even. She got half his fortune and he was made to look like a complete fool. The last I heard of her she had married a Russian Oligarch and had everything upgraded, if you know what I mean. She now looks in her early thirties and a total babe. Oh revenge is sweet." As she says it she shouts, "There it is, I knew that I never forget a face." Crowding around her we see a picture of what appears to be Stephen looking out at us. He has his arm around an older woman who must be Veronica. Like Camilla said the woman is positively glowing. He looks a bit younger and very handsome in a black dinner suit. Studying the caption Camilla reads, "Veronica Ashworthy and Joseph Cannelli." I look at Ben in surprise. He is studying the photograph intently. Boris says, "Do you think it really is the same person?" Ben says, "Well if it's not he has a twin brother. I suppose you can't rule anything out. Interesting though, thanks Camilla." Looking at us all triumphantly she says, "I always thought that I would make a good spy. I have a few stalker tendencies too so really I am wasted." Ben throws me a wicked grin. If only they knew.

The rest of the evening passes by pleasantly but I can tell that Ben is distracted and there are no prizes for guessing why. In the car on the way home we talk about what we saw. "What do you think Ben?" I say, looking thoughtfully at him. "I think that I will pass on the information and let them check it out. It won't be long before they do and then we will know for sure." After a brief silence I say, "If it is him, what do you make of it?" Ben laughs saying, "I don't think about it until I have the facts. If he is this Joseph character then we need to find out why he is posing as Stephen de Souza." Almost immediately a thought occurs to me. "Ben, a customer came into the store when you were away and also thought that Stephen was someone called Joey. He appeared annoyed and when he walked away from her I asked her about it. She said that she thought he was her boyfriend's brother but he had denied it." Nodding Ben says, "Yes, my boss told me. They didn't have anything else to go on though so couldn't find any information out." Racking my brains I try to remember the brother's name. All of a sudden I do and say, "Mikey, that was her boyfriend's name. I remember now." Ben looks interested and says, "I'll let them know. Thanks Bella, you and Camilla should team up, you would be unstoppable." He laughs and I pretend to hit him on the arm. "You never know Ben, stranger things have happened." Looking at me with a stern face he says, "Not if I have anything to do with it Bella. You are staying well away from that part of my life."

As I look out of the window I think to myself, if only we both could.

Chapter 28

I am not surprised to find myself alone the next morning when I wake up. Ben had been preoccupied all night and there are no prizes for guessing where he has gone.
As I get ready for work I think about what we found out last night. It seems that Stephen could really be this Joseph Cannelli but why would he be posing as somebody else? I have a feeling that it won't take Ben long to find out the answers though.
As soon as I get into work the security guard looks up and says, "Oh Bella, I have been told to tell you to go to Mr De Souza's office, the minute you get in. Apparently it's urgent." Smiling at him I head towards Stephen's office with trepidation. I am not sure how I will react to him after last night and I feel unnerved as to what he wants.
Reaching his office I knock hesitantly and hear him asking me to come in. As I enter he jumps up from behind his desk and I notice a worried look on his face. In surprise I can see that he is not alone. Two people are standing looking at me, their expressions grim and I feel extremely uneasy.
Stephen says in a worried voice, "I am sorry Bella but

these two officers are from the Police and they need to speak to you." In shock I ask, "Oh no is it Ben, is he Ok? Please don't say that he's been in an accident." Shaking his head Stephen says quietly, "It's not Ben Bella. I will let the officers explain but I am here if you need me." He touches my shoulder gently as he leaves the room and my legs shaking I turn to face the officers.

One of the officer's steps forward saying, "Miss Bella Brown, can you confirm that that is your name?" I nod my head and he says grimly, "I am Detective Inspector Adams and my colleague is Detective Constable Barnes. We would like you to accompany us to Guildford Police Station to answer a few questions." I am in total shock. I don't know what is going on and what they think that I can help them with. Shaking my head I say stuttering, "But why, what is it about?" Sternly Inspector Adams says, "You will know when we get to the station. I am afraid that we are going to have to insist that you accompany us." Looking at the woman officer she nods saying more gently, "You will find everything out there. Hopefully it shouldn't take long and will turn out to be a matter of routine."

They walk with me out of the room and I see Stephen pacing up and down the corridor. As he sees us he rushes over in concern. "Where are you going, what's happening?" Inspector Adams turns to him and says,

"Miss Brown needs to come to the station to answer some questions. I am sure that she will let you know when she has finished." Stephen looks at me in disbelief and I can feel my eyes welling up with tears. Concerned he says, "Don't worry Bella, I will phone Ben and get him to meet you there." Nodding unhappily I follow the officers out to the waiting car.

They don't say anything on the journey and I am totally in the dark as to what they want to speak to me about. As soon as we reach the station I am shown into what I imagine to be an interview room. Detective Barnes, who appears kinder than her colleague asks if I would like a drink. I shake my head in refusal and then they both sit down in front of me. Inspector Adams says, "Miss Brown, we have asked you here in relation to funds going missing from The Hardcastle Group of Stores. What we want to know is if you have any knowledge of this." I look at them in shock and answer in a small voice, "No, only that there is a problem that they are looking into." Inspector Adams leans forward and says, "I understand that you have close personal relations with the group's owner Mr Ben Hardcastle, is that correct?" Nodding I say, "Yes we live together." Looking at me carefully he says, "And do I understand that before your relationship you were engaged to a Mr Nathan

Matthews?" In surprise I say, "Yes, but that was ages ago." Leaning back Inspector Adams says, "And can you also confirm that you were also implicated in the crime that he was imprisoned for, namely that he planned on stealing several millions of pounds from innocent people and organisations?" Looking at him in surprise I say, "What is this. Do you think that Nathan is responsible? Surely it can't be him, he is in prison." Looking stern Inspector Adams says, "Just answer the question Miss Brown." Shaking my head I say, "Nathan was trying to set me up to take the blame for his crime, but he was found out before he could carry it out. I was otherwise not involved. I mean how could I be, I know nothing about computers and wouldn't want to commit a crime even if I could?" The two Detectives share a look and then he says, "Maybe that is what you wanted everyone to believe. Now he is out of the way you can carry on with the plan and have the money to yourself." Suddenly I feel sick. I can't believe that this is happening. Why would they think that I have anything to do with stealing money? I can see them both watching me with interest and then there is a knock on the door, interrupting the proceedings. Inspector Adams goes out and his colleague just looks at me as I sit here nervously. After a few minutes he comes back and whispers something to her. Looking at me he says, "It would appear that your boss Stephen is outside and would like to sit in on our conversation. Is that ok with you?" Looking at him in surprise I wonder how I do feel about it. After all, we are not sure if he is who he says he is. However this whole thing is so intimidating that any familiar face would be a welcome one. Seeing me nod he goes outside and is soon followed into the room by Stephen.

Racing over to me his face is a picture of concern. "It's ok Bella; I'm here to help you. I have left several messages for Ben so I will wait with you until he arrives." I look at him gratefully. I still can't believe that he is anything other than what he claims to be. He seems to have a knack of always being there when I need him and I am grateful for this at this moment as I am getting increasingly more alarmed as each minute goes by.

Pulling up his chair again Officer Adams says, "It would appear that there is unexplained activity coming from your computer Miss Brown that cannot be explained by your IT department. Can you tell us who else has access to your computer?" Surprised I say, "I suppose that anybody could come in but it is only my assistant April and I who use the office. She has her own computer though so has no need to use mine." A smile spreads across Officer Adam's face and he says, "So you are saying that only you currently log in to that particular computer." As I nod miserably, I am well aware that this just adds fuel to their theory. Stephen pipes up, "Officer, is this what you are basing this questioning on, the fact that there is strange computer activity coming from Bella's computer?" Looking surprised at the interruption the officer nods saying, "Yes it is. However we do know that the group are losing money through online transactions. After investigation by the bank they have narrowed down the only suspect activity to be coming from Miss Brown's computer, and given her association with a well known technical fraudster it all adds up quite considerably against her, don't you think?" To my surprise Stephen stands up and pulls me up with him. "Well forgive me officers but I cannot see what else there is to achieve here. Bella has told you that she knows nothing of this or any fraudulent activity on or off her computer. Therefore the rest is just speculation. Maybe when you come to us with concrete proof that she is responsible then you can ask her further questions with her solicitor present. Now if you don't mind we are busy people with jobs to go to. Come on Bella, we're leaving."

I notice that the two officers look annoyed. I am not even sure that we are allowed to leave but they don't stop us as we walk out of the room. Just before the door closes Officer Adams calls out, "Don't go far Miss

Brown. I have a feeling that this isn't the last we will be seeing of you." Looking angrily at them Stephen pulls me along beside him and doesn't stop until we are outside. Once we are a fair distance away he turns to me and says gently, "What am I going to do with you Bella? Always in trouble." Seeing my eyes fill up he reaches up to them and wipes the tears away. "Don't worry; it's obvious that they don't have anything concrete to go on. It's obviously a misunderstanding. I am sure it will soon get sorted out." Then to my surprise he pulls me against him and holds me tightly. Whispering in my ear he says, "Once again I have an overwhelming need to protect you Bella. What are we going to do about that?" I shift myself so that I am out of his grasp and look at him unsure of what to do next. All I can think of is Ben so I say, "Why hasn't Ben called you back Stephen. Did you leave a message on his phone?"

Stephen looks angry and says bitterly, "Not just one message Bella but several. I also texted him and rang his secretary. She told me that she would pass on my message but that was hours ago now and still no word. I'll say one thing for your boyfriend; he likes to disappear when you need him the most." He looks angry and annoyed and I feel put out. He knows nothing at all about Ben and shouldn't be saying these things, however something at the back of my mind is nagging at me,

where is Ben and why hasn't he called?
Noticing my expression Stephen smiles softly saying, "Come on, let's get a coffee. You are obviously in shock and need to regroup. The caffeine will do you good."
I fall in beside him and follow him to the nearest coffee shop, both of us silent and deep in our own thoughts.

Chapter 29

Sitting in the coffee shop with Stephen we must look like any other couple having lunch together. I notice lots of the women in the shop gazing enviously at me and lustfully at Stephen. He on the other hand doesn't notice any of it because he is looking at me intently and giving me his undivided attention. Anyone else would be flattered by the attention but not me. All I want is for Stephen to be Ben and I feel hurt that he hasn't called and worried at the same time. I almost can't concentrate on what Stephen is saying until leaning forward he lifts my head up to look at him. Shocked by the intimacy of the move I look at him in surprise. His eyes are staring at me and I feel mesmerised by them. Softly he says, "Earth to Bella. You are miles away. I was just saying that when you feel up to it I will drive you home. You need some time to adjust to what's happened." I pull away sharply and say, "Thanks, but I am more worried about Ben. Have you still not heard from him?" Stephen shakes his head and says, "Why don't you give him a call. He is more likely to answer if you call." Feeling stupid I wonder why I hadn't thought of that. I suppose I am so used to being told to call his secretary or Pete when he is on his other business that the thought never even crossed my mind. Stephen looks at me with interest as I rummage around in my bag for my phone. I decide to text him just in case he can't talk. I just ask him to call me urgently and I can see that Stephen looks puzzled as to why I don't just call him.

However almost immediately the phone rings and I hear Ben's voice sounding worried. "What's the matter Bella are you ok?" Feeling somewhat surprised I say, "Didn't you get Stephen's messages?" There is a short silence and then in a low voice Ben says, "Is he with you now?" I say, "Yes, but that doesn't answer my question." Ben then says quietly, "Don't react to what I say but I have received no messages from Stephen Bella, or anyone else for that matter, however I have found some things out and I need you to act normally and ask Stephen to drive you home. I know where you are and how you got there and it is important that you just carry on as you are and take him back to the house. I will meet you there in half an hour, but you mustn't let him leave." Ben's words make me feel cold inside. Something is definitely not right and Stephen is involved that much is obvious. I am puzzled as to why he needs me to take him home but trust him and will do as he says. Putting the phone back into my bag I can feel Stephen's eyes upon me and with a small smile say, "He says that his phone was out of charge and he hasn't had time to look at his messages. He can't talk now as he is in a meeting." I notice that Stephen looks angry and he says, "Well I hope that he is more supportive when he finds out what you have been through today. I'm sorry Bella, I know that he's my boss and your boyfriend but I am not impressed. You deserve better than this. Some things are more important than work and he had better wake up to that fact otherwise he may lose you to someone more deserving who would take care of you a darned sight better than he does." Willing myself not to react I just shrug saying, "I'm sorry Stephen but I have had an awful day and if it's not too much trouble would you be able to give me a lift home?" The angry look disappears and Stephen says gently, "Of course Bella. Let's go and find my car and I'll get you home. A rest is definitely what you need." As we drive home Stephen tries to keep my spirits up by reassuring me about what happened today. I am grateful for his help and am actually quite fearful of what I am about to find out. Coupled with the visit to the Police Station I have never felt so anxious. Luckily Stephen thinks that my concern is solely related to the incident at the Police Station and so is oblivious to anything that may concern him.

Before long we reach the house and turning to Stephen I say, "Thank you Stephen. I really appreciate your help today. The fact that you were there made a stressful situation easier to bear." His eyes soften and he reaches over and places his hand on my arm. "Like I said Bella, I have this overwhelming need to protect you for some reason. It really was my pleasure." Mustering a smile I say, "Let me thank you by offering you a drink. It's the least I can do." Stephen smiles and follows me into the house.

We are soon in the kitchen and I can feel him watching me carefully as I make us some drinks. It feels strange knowing that something is about to happen and I can't help feeling somehow guilty about what may happen next. Sensing that I am preoccupied Stephen says, "I'm sorry Bella I know I shouldn't but I am going to say this anyway." Turning towards him in surprise I watch as he covers the short amount of distance that there is between us. Standing before me he reaches out and pulls me to him. I try to move away but he tightens his grip and pulls my face up to meet his. "Bella, I can feel that there is something between us. You may not know it but I do. I have been watching you and know that you are not happy. Something is wrong with your relationship and I don't think that you have faced up to it yet." Quickly I shake my head, "You've got it wrong Stephen, I love Ben, and there is nothing wrong with our relationship." Still holding on he says softly, "Perhaps not with you but

I recognise the signs in him. He is always away and can't seem to be contacted. You appear on edge and there are stories flying around about him and another woman. Face up to it Bella, he is playing around and I can't watch you get hurt. Let me take care of you, come with me now and we can walk away from all of this. I love you and want to care for you and I know that I could make you happy." Then before I can answer he leans towards me and kisses me with such passion that I am totally taken by surprise. Before he even finishes we suddenly hear, "If I were you I would move away from my girlfriend or it will be the last thing you ever do." Pulling away sharply Stephen spins around and as he does so I can see Ben standing in the kitchen looking thunderous. If looks could kill then Stephen would be dead already. At any moment I expect to see Ben race over and punch Stephen such is the animosity in his expression, but then I notice that he is not alone. Standing behind him in the doorway, looking at me with such hatred is the unmistakeable figure of Vanessa Montague.

Chapter 30

At first there is total silence as we all stare at each other in shock. Then Ben says in a cold angry voice, "I think that the two of you owe us an explanation." Looking at Stephen in confusion I am surprised to see the flicker of a triumphant expression cross his face, and then it is gone as quickly as it appeared and is replaced by one of indifference. I go to speak but Ben holds up his hand and looking towards me his expression softens and he says, "Not you Bella, I am talking to Stephen and Vanessa." As he says the words I notice a look pass between them and then Stephen quickly says, "What are you talking about Ben?" I notice that Vanessa stays silent but her angry look has been replaced by one of wariness.

We all stare at Ben in confusion and then he moves over to where I am standing and pulls me beside him. Looking angrily at the others he says, "You may as well tell us everything otherwise I won't be responsible for my actions." I am now extremely confused and as I look over to where Vanessa is standing I can see her lip quiver and she looks down at the floor. I notice that she is quite petite in build with long dark hair. She has a fragile air about her and I can understand why Ben has always wanted to protect her. Then in surprise I see Stephen walk over to her and put his arm around her gently. He looks at Ben and me with a guilty expression and says, "Leave Vanessa out of this. She hasn't done anything wrong."

Turning to look at him I see her expression soften and she says quietly, "It's ok Stephen. They deserve to know the truth." I can still feel Ben tense beside me and I look between them all not understanding what on earth is going on. Vanessa moves forward and then looks at me with a hard expression. Addressing her words towards Ben she says, "I'm sorry Ben. As you have already guessed I have had you on a bit of a wild goose chase. I am afraid that I had to get you out of the way so that Stephen could find out what I asked him to."

She carries on tentatively. "Stephen came to me a few months ago and told me something that worried me. It concerned your new girlfriend Bella and the more I heard the more worried I got." Now I am very confused. I look at Stephen and he looks back at me almost apologetically. Carrying on Vanessa says, "Stephen told me that he had heard that Bella was plotting with her boyfriend Nathan Matthews to steal millions of pounds using your organisation as a cover. If they succeeded then the stores would be bankrupt and you would be ruined. She on the other hand would flee to another country with the proceeds where she would wait for Nathan to be released." As she says the words I still can't take in what she is saying.

Moving nearer to Ben Vanessa says, "I will do anything for you Ben, you know that and I couldn't just stand by and let her ruin you and break your heart at the same time. You mean too much to me for me to allow that to happen and so I readily agreed with Stephen's plan." I go to speak, angry at what I am hearing but Ben puts his hand in mine and squeezes it saying, "Carry on Vanessa." Looking at me once again with anger Vanessa says, "We arranged for Simon's wife to receive a promotion that she couldn't refuse which would open up a position in the store that would give Stephen the access he needed. With the full backing of my bank we taught him everything that he needed to know and then laid a fake trail for you to follow Ben to keep you away long enough to install him in the position and for him to get to work finding the proof we needed. Stephen was to expose Bella as the manipulative thief that she is which would open your eyes to the monster that you had become besotted by." Now I am extremely angry. "How dare you come here and tell all these lies." I shout, not caring that Ben wants me to be quiet. "I haven't done anything wrong and I love Ben and would never hurt him." Vanessa glowers at me and Ben says, "So

Stephen, tell us where you got your information from." Stephen has the grace to look embarrassed and says, "A while ago my brother contacted me asking me to visit him. He said that it was urgent and that I must go." Hesitating he says, "My brother is in prison and as it turns out befriended Bella's ex boyfriend Nathan Matthews." Suddenly I understand where this is going and I sink down on to the nearby settee. I knew it was Nathan, not for sure but deep down inside it had to be him. Looking concerned Stephen says, "My brother and I have never got on and I was surprised when I received the visiting order. I suppose that curiosity got the better of me and I went along to see what he wanted. He told me that Nathan and Bella were planning on stealing vast sums of money and that her relationship with Ben had just been a cover up. He told me that a friend of his knew Vanessa Montague who had told him that she had a soft spot for Ben and would probably pay good money for the information that we had. He wanted me to find her and get a large sum of money from her in return for saving her beloved Ben and the stores that he knew the Bank partly owned." Stephen hesitates and looks at Vanessa. She smiles at him and says, "Don't worry tell him the rest. He needs to know." Intrigued I listen as Stephen says, "What Mikey didn't know was that I already knew Vanessa. We have known each other for a while and so I told her of their plan. Between us we hatched our own plan to expose Bella and Nathan and get them out of Ben's life for good." Then Stephen looks at me and his face softens. "The more I discovered about Bella the more I began to realise that my brother must be wrong. I found no evidence at all linking her to anything and her love for Ben was obvious. However I couldn't explain how the money was leaking from the stores. Vanessa was still convinced as it appeared that our investigations always led back to Bella's computer. So she decided to hand it over to the police so that they could find out once and for all."

As he finishes I look at them both in disbelief. Ben is looking thoughtful and as I catch his eye he smiles at me reassuringly. Turning towards me he says, "Bella, make us all a drink will you. I have a feeling that this is going to be a long night." We all look at him in surprise and he says, "Right sit down everyone. Let's start from the beginning."

Chapter 31

Once I have made the drinks we all sit around and Ben runs through everything again and again. We soon establish that Vanessa was acting out of concern for Ben and Stephen out of concern for her. I am still confused though and say, "I don't understand. What was Nathan hoping to achieve by telling these lies?" Ben says, "I would think that if he could prove that you were taking the money it would give him grounds to appeal and could be released from prison. He would get his revenge on us by sending you to prison in his place and ruin me in the process. What I still want to know though is how he is still stealing the money and where is it going?" Looking around at the blank faces I can tell that nobody knows. Suddenly Ben looks at Stephen saying, "I think that you had also better explain who you really are." Stephen looks at Vanessa and she nods encouragingly. "He probably already knows, it doesn't matter." Looking at us both Stephen says, "My name is not Stephen De Souza it is Joseph Cannelli. Vanessa arranged for my new identity for the purposes of my new job. She knew that the real Stephen de Souza was currently away for a while and his background was a perfect fit for what we needed. The plan was that by the time he returned we would have finished the job." Once again he hesitates and in surprise I see Vanessa reach out and take his hand. Turning to face us she says, "I have known Joseph for a while now. He has helped me out from time to time by accompanying me to various functions and parties. We have grown close over our time together and I trust him and value his friendship greatly. He is nothing like his brother and deserves to get on in life. For my part he fills a part of my life that would otherwise go unfulfilled. I am lucky to have him as a friend and like Ben I would do anything for him."

I can tell that Ben is not surprised. He probably knew it all already. I am still amazed at the revelations though. I would never have believed what I have heard this evening and it is taking a lot for it to sink in.

Ben then says, "Well, at least we all know now what we have to do. As you can tell Vanessa, Bella is no threat to me at all. It would appear that not for the first time she is being set up to take the blame for Nathan's criminal activity. Stephen, I understand why you have done what you have but if I catch you touching my girlfriend again I will not hold back a second time." Stephen grins guiltily at me and says, "I'm sorry Bella, Ben. I hope that you don't think too badly of me." Carrying on Ben says, "Vanessa, I know that you have got my best interests at heart and you know that I love you. Nothing has changed there but your methods could have been better. Now we know where we're at the next step is to find out where the money is going and how we can pin it all back on to Nathan. Any ideas?" There is silence as we all think about the situation. Stephen then says, "I do know that Mikey wanted me to get Bella away from Ben as proof to Nathan that Ben was suffering. Apparently as soon as they had split up he could finish the job." Looking thoughtful Ben says, "What do you think that means, can you find out?" Stephen says, "I'll try but the easiest thing would be for them to think that their plan had worked. Then we may find out what he has in store next." I don't like the way this is going and look desperately at Ben. He looks at me softly and then pulls me against him, kissing my hair. "We'll think of something Bella, don't worry." Turning to the others he says, "I think that we should call it a night now. Stephen take Vanessa home and I'll be in touch. We will work out a plan to finish this once and for all."

As they get up to leave Vanessa looks sheepishly at us both. Looking at me she says in a small voice, "I am sorry Bella for what I have put you through. I really thought that you were the bad guy and I couldn't let you destroy Ben. He means the world to me and I wouldn't stand by and do nothing." I can tell that she means every word but I can also recognise that their relationship goes beyond that of sexual attraction. It is a deep friendship and loyalty and I cannot judge her because I would do the same thing in her position. Smiling at her I say, "I know Vanessa. You don't have to explain."

Stephen takes her hand and I watch as Ben goes with them to the door. I feel a little happier now but something inside of me knows that this is just the beginning and it fills me with dread.

When Ben returns he takes me in his arms and I can feel his heart beating. In an emotional voice he says, "The sight of you in his arms as he kissed you will live with me forever. I could have killed him then and there." Pulling back he looks angrily into my eyes and says, "You are mine Bella, you always were and always will be. Nothing will ever come between us and I will destroy anyone that tries. When I think of what they have put you through it makes me want to hurt them." Lifting my fingers I stroke the side of his face. "I love you Ben and nobody else. Nothing ever will come between us, I won't let it. Now enough talking for one night." Leaning towards him I kiss him gently and then he crushes me to him, his fingers entwined in my hair as he hold my head firmly and kisses me until my legs go weak with desire. Sweeping me up into his arms he carries me upstairs. Everything else can wait until tomorrow.

Chapter 32

I didn't get much sleep last night and neither did Ben. I couldn't sleep as the events of the day played out in my mind. Half way through the night Ben had gone downstairs to his study and I knew that he was also thinking of what had happened.

Over breakfast he notices my worried expression. "What's wrong Bella?" he says gently, "Are you worrying about it all?" Sighing I say, "Yes, I can't help it. What if the police come back today and arrest me? I could go to prison for something that I didn't do." To my surprise Ben smiles and coming over to me he pulls me against him. Hugging me tightly he says, "You don't have to worry about that Bella." Before he can explain there is a knock on the door and I look at him in surprise. "Who on earth could that be at this time?" Shrugging Ben goes off to answer the door and in no time at all he is back, and my heart sinks at the sight of the two police officers following him. Smiling reassuringly at me Ben says, "The officers would like a word Bella." He then comes over and stands next to me gripping my hand tightly as we face them.

Inspector Adams is looking at me with a stern expression and officer Barnes looks uncomfortable. Clearing his throat Inspector Adams says, "We are sorry to intrude so early on in the day but thought that you would like to hear sooner rather than later." Gripping Ben's hand tightly I say anxiously, "What is it?" The Inspector looks annoyed and says, "We are here to tell you Miss Brown that we are no longer considering you as a suspect in our investigations." I look up at Ben in shock and notice that he is looking at the officers and raises his eyes as if waiting for them to carry on. Clearing his throat the Inspector shifts awkwardly on his feet and says, "And we would like to offer you our most sincere apologies for detaining you yesterday which we understand would have caused you considerable distress which was unnecessary." Now I am totally confused. How can things have changed so quickly in such a short space of time? I don't really know what to say and Ben says, "Well that's a relief isn't it Bella. Thank you both for coming, I'll show you out." Ben follows them out of the room and I sink back down into my chair in shock and relief. Thank goodness for that. When Ben comes back he winks at me and says, "Happy now Bella?" Suddenly I know who was responsible for this visit and looking gratefully at him I say, "You arranged that didn't you." Laughing Ben shakes his head saying, "No, not me Bella. However I do luckily have friends in some very high places. All it took was a phone call from them and

as you can see it all goes away." I know that Ben is referring to his boss. Once again I wonder just what it is that they do and how far up the chain they really go.
As Ben turns to make us a drink I say, "Ben, you never did tell me how everything came about yesterday. How did you find out that Vanessa was involved with Stephen?" Laughing Ben says, "Again Bella, I can't take the credit for that. Luckily there are many people working for the organisation whose job it is to put the jigsaw pieces together. As soon as I found out I went to Vanessa and brought her here. I knew that I had to have the element of surprise, that way they couldn't work out their story in advance." Remembering the events in this kitchen yesterday I feel uncomfortable and say, "You know that I never kissed Stephen back don't you? It came as a complete surprise to me and then you were here." Ben looks angry again and says grimly, "That kiss was all part of the plan. He must have heard the car pull up and wanted me to find you in a compromising position. As they said, the plan was to split us up. They both don't know of my other job and I can certainly spot the signs, I've used them myself in the past. Classic seduction techniques. If I didn't know better I would have thought that they worked for the organisation."
I don't like to picture Ben in that world, doing the same things that Stephen did. Seeing my face fall Ben lifts my

face towards his and says softly, "Not since I met you again Bella. That part of my life is over for good. I can't change the past but you are my future and it doesn't involve playing games anymore, no matter how high the stakes may be."

Thinking about his previous life makes me realise just how much Ben is giving up for me. I want to ask him so much more about it but I am afraid that I won't like what I hear.

Changing the subject I suddenly laugh saying, "I never once thought that Stephen was Vanessa's boyfriend though. I mean the girl that I met said that she had heard that Joey, as she called him, had a rich girlfriend but I never connected the two." Ben suddenly smiles and says, "Stephen is not Vanessa's boyfriend Bella, he never was." Looking at him in confusion I see him laugh as the truth dawns on me, "What, are you saying that Stephen is a male prostitute?" Laughing Ben says, "Not exactly Bella, but that is quite funny. Stephen or should I say Joseph is what is called a high class escort. We did some digging and with what Clarissa told us and then finding out about his association with Vanessa it didn't take us long to track down the agency that he works for."

Ben laughs at the expression on my face. I am totally gob smacked. Ben carries on. "Rich ladies pay good looking men to accompany them to functions and dinners. The more attractive the better, there is quite a lot of cutting out stakes at these events. Usually their husbands have left them or are having affairs and the wives need a boost. If they are lucky the escort may offer other services if he likes them enough and I have known several ladies, Vanessa included who just use the services of these men rather than have a complicated relationship." I'm afraid to ask but I say, "You seem to know a lot about it Ben, you weren't…?" Laughing Ben says, "Of course not. Although don't judge them Bella. They do a great job and do these women no end of good. I usually find that the women adore their escorts and forge quite a strong bond with them, as you can see with Vanessa and Stephen. He obviously cares for her deeply; you can see it in the way he is around her. I can't find fault with him because he was only doing what she asked thinking that he was helping her." Thinking about it I can see that Ben is right. Stephen was only doing what he thought was right and I shouldn't judge them.

As Ben hands me my coffee I say, "What happens now, where do we go from here?" Taking a sip of his drink Ben says, "That's what we're about to find out. As soon as you are ready Bella, I'm taking you to work with me. As I look at his expression I know that he isn't referring to the stores and I am gripped with a sudden excitement.

Chapter 33

Ben drives us to London. He doesn't say much in the car and I am overwhelmed with excitement. Finally I am going to find out about the part of him that I know nothing about. I wonder what I will discover. I have images of secret rooms filled with computer equipment and gadgetry. I have seen enough James Bond films to feed my imagination and I can't wait.
We drive up to the River Thames and approach what I know to be the MI5 building. Looking over at Ben I can see that he is relaxed but deep in thought. I on the other hand almost can't contain my excitement and shift nervously in my seat. Noticing this Ben smiles and says, "Don't be too disappointed Bella, it's not what you think." Feeling my heart sink I hope that he is wrong. I want it to be everything that I think and more.
Ben drives into an underground car park and the barrier comes down behind us. He parks and we leave the car and head towards a lift at the end of the car park. I feel vaguely disappointed that the cars all look ordinary. No Aston Martins or Porches here; this is not looking good. Holding my hand in the lift Ben squeezes it and says, "Are you ok Bella?" Nodding I almost can't breathe with

excitement. He laughs and says, "I wish that I was responsible for your flushed cheeks and shining eyes Bella. Like I said though, it's not what you think."
Before I can reply the lift reaches its destination and we step outside into a large reception. There are many people milling around and Ben takes me over to the reception desk at which sits a pretty receptionist. Smiling warmly at us she says, "Hi Ben, how are you today?" He returns the smile and says, "Fine thank you Katie, I need to sign a visitor in." Katie looks at me with interest saying, "Of course. Please sign in here and I will get you a visitor's badge."
I do as I am told and once we have the badge Ben takes me to another lift. This time we are not alone and I look with interest at the workers who share the space with us. Again they look ordinary enough and images of spies sporting guns and secret weapons seem very far away from this lot.
We get out at the 3rd floor and walk down a clinical corridor that houses several doors. Reaching one at the end Ben knocks and then we go inside.
I can see that it is a meeting room. There is a large table around which are several chairs. The large windows look out over the River Thames and there is a water cooler in the corner. Apart from that the room is sparse and certainly doesn't house the command centre that I was

expecting to see. There is nobody in the room and Ben says, "Take a seat Bella, I'll go and find the others. I won't be long." Kissing me on the top of my head he leaves me in the clinical room and goes elsewhere. Moving over to the window I look out at the scene outside. London fascinates me. It is always so busy and the view is amazing. The River Thames is a hive of activity and I notice the various landmarks with interest. Red busses and black taxis speed over the bridge and the people look like an army of ants going about their business.

I am interrupted by the door opening and looking around I see Ben coming back accompanied by his boss and Pete.

His boss smiles briefly at me and says, "Morning Bella, I hope that you have recovered after your ordeal yesterday." This woman intimidates me so much that I can only nod nervously. I look over at Pete and he winks reassuringly. "Hi Bella," is all he says and they take a seat. Ben holds out a chair for me and I sit down next to him wondering what they are going to say.

Looking at us with a hard expression Ben's boss says, "Well here we are again. Not for the first time Nathan Matthews is causing trouble and we need to resolve it once and for all. It would appear that even from prison he can control the computers at the store. But before we can shut them down we need to recover the stolen money and prove that it is him who is the perpetrator." Looking around at us all she continues. "We have enough photographic evidence that Vanessa and Stephen have collected to prove that Bella and Stephen were having an affair." This I wasn't expecting to hear and in shock look at Ben who smiles saying. "Bella, your meetings with Stephen weren't by chance. They were carefully planned and designed to tell a different story to the one that they really did. Vanessa had arranged for a photographer to follow you both and every little hug, touch and gesture was captured. The night at the hotel was meticulously recorded, as well as the visits to the gym and the restaurant. All of this was designed to show proof to me that you were having an affair and then for Stephen to show his brother, thus convincing Nathan at the same time. We would split up and Nathan would have achieved part of his revenge." Shaking I look over at them all. I can't believe that someone had been following me all of this time. Pete adds, "We were also following Stephen and it didn't take us long to find out what was happening. After some digging we discovered who he really was and his connection to Vanessa. Ben was to be otherwise occupied to enable Stephen to carry out his plan and it didn't take him long to realise that there was nothing untoward happening at the bank.

Vanessa also wanted to put doubt in your mind Bella about Ben's fidelity hence the public appearances together which fuelled the rumours and speculation. It would also give Stephen more of a chance to comfort you and get close to you when you were at your most vulnerable."

Ben's boss then looks at us all saying, "So now we have to finish it. Stephen will be visiting his brother today with the evidence that he needs. However this alone will not be enough to convince Nathan. We need him to be 100% certain that his plan has worked and so that is where we need your help Bella." Feeling my face fall I hope that they don't expect me to leave Ben again and pretend to be with Stephen. I don't think that I could face doing that again. Ben reaches over and squeezes my hand. "It's nothing to worry about Bella. We tried to think about whom Nathan would trust the most without any doubts at all on hearing the news. The only people that visit him are his parents and so we need you to tell your parents that we have had problems and you don't think that we can resolve them. They need to think that we have split up and knowing their close relationship with Nathan's parents it won't take long for the news to get back to him from the very people that he knows wouldn't lie to him. As soon as he is convinced he will make his next move."

I can see them all looking at me with interest. Looking around at them I know that this is the best option. All I have to do is convince my parents. Something occurs to me though and I say, "But how will we know what he is planning next? I mean so far nobody knows how he is stealing the money and I can't believe that he will tell anyone. For all I know it will all come back on me again and I will be arrested." Ben's boss says, "You won't be arrested Bella you can be assured of that. You will technically be working for us and we are very protective of our operatives. I can see Ben's expression tighten and know that he isn't happy at the thought that I am being dragged in to this world. I know that it's necessary though and vow to play my part in all of this. Once again looking at his boss I say, "Can you trust Stephen though? Maybe he is closer to this than you think. I mean he went to Vanessa and told her about it all in the first place. Maybe he is the one stealing the money and has planned all of this to disguise his involvement." With surprise I notice a smile on Ben's boss's face. Her eyes shining she laughs saying, "I wish that you would reconsider working for me Bella. With training I could make you a good operative." Looking mischievously at Ben she adds, "I could have a dream team with you two. Oh the possibilities are endless." Looking cross Ben says, "In your dreams, you know the score, don't push your luck."

I am amazed at hearing the way he speaks to her. I have never heard anyone answer her back and look at them both in surprise. Pete grins and their boss laughs saying, "Sorry, couldn't resist it Ben. Yes I know, you have made your feelings very clear. Anyway getting back to your question about Stephen Bella. It is true that we are taking a gamble on trusting him. However we have found out that he is an honest guy. Everybody that knows him speaks highly of him and we can find no evidence of any criminal activity, unlike his brother. We have discovered that he had a difficult childhood and has distanced himself from his family wanting to do well for himself. He has always conducted himself well and in his spare time has been studying computers in the hope of setting up his own business. I think that we can trust him as it is well documented that he hates his brother and offers him no loyalty at all." Looking thoughtful she adds. "You are right though. We don't know what his next move will be. It is unlikely that there is anyone with which he will share his plans and the only thing we can do is to monitor the computer activity and try to crack his system."

As I listen to her my mind is working away thinking about the problems that face us. Above anyone else in this room I know Nathan the best, or at least I once thought so. There is one person who he would trust though and I can't believe that I haven't thought of it before now.

Turning to face them all I say, "I do know one person who he may confide in." I notice Ben's boss sit up and look at me with interest. Ben and Pete also look surprised and I say, "It may not be feasible but the one person that Nathan is desperate for news of and totally obsessed with is Melissa."

I notice a look pass between the three of them which I can't quite fathom. There is a brief silence and then Ben's boss says, "Why do you say that Bella?" Looking directly at her I say, "My mother mentioned when I last saw her that Nathan was desperate for news of her. Apparently he has asked his parents to track her down and she is all he can think of. When I last saw him at the Lodge he told me that she was his soul mate, his perfect match in every way and they were going away together to start a new life. He didn't know that she wasn't who she said she was and I would think that if he was to hear from her it wouldn't take him long to tell her everything."

Once again Ben's boss laughs. "Thank you Bella, you have been a great help. I will think about what you have said but it may not be as easy as you think. Melissa is currently unavailable to help us out and we may need to think of another way. For the time being though you need to visit your parents today. As soon as we get started this can be resolved. Pete, I need you to step up the computer problem. Use whoever you need to monitor the system and look for every possibility. Ben, you need to do as we discussed and hopefully it won't be long before we can all forget about Nathan Matthews once and for all."

She then pushes back her chair and standing up she looks at me thoughtfully. "Thank you Bella. I am sorry to have to involve you again. If you can think of anything at all no matter how small or insignificant you may think it please tell either Pete or Ben. Now I must go, I have a busy day ahead and I am sure that you do too." Smiling warmly at me Pete follows her out of the room, leaving Ben and I to think about what she has said.

Ben goes to stand up but I pull him back down beside me. Looking at me in surprise I say to him, "What has she asked you to do Ben?" I am fearful of his answer but I have to know. Sighing he says, "I have to go back to the London flat until this has been sorted out. Once again I have to be seen out with Vanessa to reinforce our break up. You can stay at home but I am afraid that I can't come back until this is over. We can speak on the phone but they have to be new phones that can't be traced to us."

My heart sinking I knew that this was probably going to be the case. Pulling me around to look at him Ben says softly, "I hate it as much as you do Bella. Please trust me though. You know that I would never do anything to hurt you, it's just a means to an end." Nodding miserably I know he is right. As hard as it is going to be it's not going to be forever. I will play my part in it all and not cause a fuss. I am not going to let Nathan win; it's time we fought back.

Chapter 34

Ben and I decided that the sooner I tell my parents the better. We spent the evening together and made sure that we didn't speak about what had to happen next. As I remember the events of last night though my heart sinks. We spent the whole night in bed, making the most of our last night together. I have to keep telling myself that it will be over soon. The thought that he has gone away again is unbearable. At this moment I hate Nathan more than I ever thought was possible. Even though he hasn't succeeded in his aim to break Ben and I up, in a small way he has, as we cannot be together until this is all resolved. Thinking about Ben spending time with Vanessa doesn't worry me anymore. I can see that they have a deep bond which despite my questions Ben won't talk much about.

He did warn me about Stephen though. I laugh as I remember his words as he left. "I don't trust him one bit with you Bella. I know that everyone says he was just doing his job but I am not convinced. If he lays one finger on you tell me and I will come straight back and they will just have to deal with the consequences. Seeing him all over you twice in our Kitchen was enough to make me kill him if he tries it a third time." Personally I don't think that Stephen or should I call him Joseph now? I am so confused, did have any other agenda other than what he was asked to do.

As I drive into my parent's driveway my heart sinks. I am not looking forward to this visit at all. Deceiving my Parents is not going to come easy to me and I can't wait for it all to be over.
With a heavy heart I knock on my parent's door. The door flies open and my mother stands there beaming at me. However her smile soon fades as she notices my worried expression. "Oh my God Bella, what's the matter? Come in and tell me. It's not Ben is it?" As she says the words I can't help it and burst out crying. Not for the reasons that she thinks but because of the guilt I am feeling on deceiving her. Putting her arm around me she guides me into the kitchen and flicks the kettle on. Handing me a tissue she says, "Now now, I will make us a nice cup of tea and you can tell me all about it."
As she fusses around me I relay the story as we agreed. My voice trembling I say, "Ben and I have had a huge argument. He accused me of having an affair with my new boss whilst he was away." Seeing my mum's horrified expression I quickly continue. "But that's not all. Phoebe told me that there were rumours that Ben was

seeing an old flame of his whilst he was away. He denies it but I am not so sure. He has been very distant lately and I just put it down to the stress of work, but now I am wondering if it was due to this other woman." Now the words are out I feel even more terrible than before, especially as my mum rushes over and hugs me tightly, tears streaming down her face. "You poor thing. How could he do this to you? I always thought that he was a good un. You must come home and stay with us until this blows over." Tears still pouring down my cheeks I say, "No, there's no need. Ben has returned to London to give us time to think. I will be fine at home but I just needed someone to talk to." Still holding me my mum says, "And who better than your own mother. There there it will all sort itself out in the end, these things usually do." Sniffing I say in a small voice, "I am not sure that they can be this time. Why do I always pick men that mess me around?" Nodding in agreement my mother suddenly looks nervous and says, "I'm sorry to ask Bella but is any of this true about you and your new boss? I hate to ask but you are a beautiful young lady and it wouldn't surprise me at all if he was taken with you." Shaking my head I reply, "He has been paying me a lot of attention and I suppose it could look bad, but there is nothing in it at all, there is no relationship." My mum carries on making the drinks and I can tell that her mind is processing the information. I feel drained and incredibly guilty at lying to her; I just hope that this will all be resolved soon.

I decide not to stay long. Now that I have kept my part of the bargain I just want to get away from it all for five minutes. My mum promises to fill my Dad in and I hope that she doesn't waste any time in telling Nathan's mother. I promise to keep in touch and rather hastily refuse her kind information to come and stay with me. That is one complication that I can definitely do without. Waving at her as I drive off I decide to pull over and call Ben as soon as I am out of sight. I use the new phone and he answers immediately. "Bella, are you ok?" Sighing I say, "I think so. I have just told my mother the story so hopefully it won't be long before she spreads the word. How about you, how are you bearing up?" In a weary voice he says, "Trying to but not succeeding very well. I have moved back into the flat and it feels like a lonely place to be. I wish that you were here with me and the thought that I don't even know when we can be together again is driving me mad." "I know Ben. This is getting to be a habit now. You would think that it would be easy now but somehow it feels even harder than the last time." I picture Ben holding the phone close to his mouth and say huskily, "The thought of your mouth so close to mine over the airwaves is so distracting. I wish that I could reach into the phone and kiss you right now." I hear him gasp and a low moan escapes him. "Don't Bella; this is hard enough as it is. If you carry on I'll be home before you at this rate." Laughing to myself I lighten the tone. "Anyway, I am heading home via the fish and chip shop and then I am going to have an evening of me time, just me, the food, a bottle of wine and a chick flick. Oh and after a nice deep bubble bath with candles, where I will lay back and dream of you." As I hear him groan in desperation again I laugh saying softly, "Good night Ben, and sweet dreams." Hanging up I feel a little better. At least this time we can have some form of communication, even if it is in cyber space.

Chapter 35

A few days pass and life carries on as normal. I have spoken to my mum on the phone several times but I still don't know if she has told Nathan's parents. I speak to Ben on the phone but he has no news from his end. I haven't seen Stephen and wonder what he is up to. The last I heard was that he was going to see his brother with the evidence that Ben and I had split up. Otherwise I have carried on as normal.

As I head off to the staff canteen with April we suddenly see Stephen walking towards us. I feel awkward as I haven't seen him since that day in my kitchen and am not sure how to act with him. As he approaches I can feel April tense up beside me and he looks at us both, his eyes appearing to bear right through us. Feeling myself flushing an amused look comes over his face and his mouth twitches in amusement. "Ladies, how nice to see my favourite homewares team." April blushes and looks to the ground and I just look at him as though he is my boss saying, "Hello Stephen, how are you?" Holding my gaze he looks at me as if he can see right through me, thoughts and all and says lazily. "Very well thank you Bella. I am glad that I have seen you. Would you mind passing by my office before you go home today. There is something that I need to discuss with you. It won't take long so just a few minutes after work will be fine." Looking at him in surprise I just nod, wondering what he has to say. Smiling at us both in farewell he leaves us and April lets out her breath saying, "I'm sorry Bella but he is so damned hot. I can't think straight around him and I don't know how on earth you can string a sentence together when he asks you something. My mind just goes blank and all I can think of is that I want is to rip his clothes off and have wild sex with him." This sets me off laughing hysterically. April never speaks like this about anyone and it is so out of character that I am totally shocked. Grinning wickedly at me and blushing profusely she says, "Well, a girl can dream can't she?" Giggling like two school girls we head off to lunch.

Later on I decide that I should tell Ben what is happening and go outside to phone him. Strangely there is no answer so I text him instead, telling him that I saw Stephen and that he wanted to see me later. I would fill him in when I speak to him.

Feeling unnerved I carry on with my day, checking my phone every five minutes just in case he calls or texts me.

By the time 5.30pm comes there is still no word from him. April heads off home and I go to find out what Stephen wants. Again I am feeling nervous as I am not

sure how to act around him.
As I reach his office I try to blank out everything that Ben has told me about him and keep a professional manner. I knock hesitantly, part of me wishing that he isn't here. My heart sinks as I hear him say, "Come in." Pushing the door open I see him sitting at his desk, papers strewn everywhere. As I approach he looks up and I see a sudden flash of uncertainty in his expression before it is replaced by the usual impenetrable gaze.
I notice that he quickly checks his watch and then says, "Take a seat Bella, I won't keep you long." Intrigued I sit down and watch him with interest as he shuffles his papers together and places them in a manila folder. He finishes something on his computer before switching it off and tidies his desk, all the time not saying a word, then he flicks his phone on to the answering service. Once he has finished he looks steadily at me and says, "Do you have plans this evening Bella?" His question takes me by surprise and I shake my head saying, "No, just a night in front of the television, why?" His expression gives nothing away and he says seriously, "I wondered if you might help me with something. It's um not strictly above board though so before I tell you what it is you must decide whether or not you want to get involved. The trouble is I am not sure that I can do it without your help." Now I am consumed with curiosity.

There is no way that I am going to refuse as now I want to know what he has in mind more than anything." Looking steadily back at him I say, "I am intrigued. As long as it is not criminal then I will help you out, if I can." Looking relieved he says quietly, "Then you must do as I say." Once again he looks at his watch and says, "Right then, we will go back to your office before the store empties and they close up for the night. Leave everything here; you can help me carry my equipment." Now I am totally intrigued. I wonder what on earth it is about but before I can ask he thrusts a black case at me to hold. It is fairly heavy and is the size of a briefcase. I watch as he grabs two more similar ones and a backpack from underneath his desk. Beckoning me to follow him he says quietly, "If anyone asks us anything let me do the talking, ok?" I nod in agreement and follow him out of his office and down the corridor towards the lift. He doesn't offer an explanation and I wonder what on earth it is all about.

Luckily we don't see anyone that we know, just the last few customers heading towards the exits. It doesn't take us long and we are soon back at my office. Stephen puts the cases on the floor and then to my surprise closes the door, locking it behind him. Noticing my surprised look he holds his finger up to his lips and says in a whisper,

"I'll explain in a minute. We haven't got much time." I watch him unpack the cases one by one. They all contain computers and various other items of an electronic nature. He works quickly and silently, hooking the computers up to both mine and April's. I notice that he keeps on looking at his watch and every time that I go to speak he silences me by holding his finger to his lips. It takes him about half an hour and then once again he looks at his watch. Crossing the room towards me he leans over and whispers, "Any minute now the security guards will do their rounds. They mustn't know that we are here. I'll explain later but you must stay silent despite what you hear." I don't trust myself to speak; this is not at all what I was expecting. As I look at him in shock and confusion he smiles gently. "Don't worry Bella; I'll explain everything when the coast is clear. Just trust me, everything will be ok."

We sit in my office in silence, just looking at each other. I can just hear the clock ticking on the wall behind us and the tension in the room is palpable. Feeling extremely stressed I just want to pace up and down. What if we get caught in here, the security guards would wonder what is going on. I am not sure if it's because I feel stressed or because it's dusty but I can feel a sneeze coming. At the same time we hear the distinct footsteps of the security guard approaching in the corridor outside.

Suddenly the door handle turns but because the door is locked the guard cannot get in. I hear him call out, "Is anybody there?" Looking at Stephen in panic I gesture to him that I am about to sneeze. Alarm registers on his face and before I know what is happening he covers the distance between us and holds his fingers underneath my nose. Then to my utter shock he pulls me towards him and kisses me with so much passion that I can't think straight. The kiss goes on and on for ages. I feel his heart beating through the thin fabric of his shirt. His tongue is moving around my mouth, caressing mine and twisting and turning assaulting my senses and leaving me shocked to the core. After what seems like an eternity he pulls away and looks sheepishly at me. He whispers, "Forgive me Bella. It's the only way I know to counteract a sneeze. It must be the surprise element that shifts the brain's focus." Still in shock I realise that I no longer have the urge to sneeze. How on earth did he discover that little trick? "What about the security guard, he might come back?" Grinning guiltily he says, "I think the coast is clear now. I'll explain everything shortly but we really need to get these computers fired up. We can't log on as they need to be untouched, but I need to connect them to my laptops." I watch as he logs in to his system and then starts putting in various codes and information which I assume must link the computers.

Both April's and mine are still turned off and I wonder what on earth he is doing. Once he has finished he sinks back in his chair and lets out a deep breath. Turning to face me he says, "Right then. I expect that you want to know what on earth is going on." I know that my face must look a picture as he laughs and reaching for his backpack he pulls out a bottle of water and throws it to me. "Drink up Bella, it could be a long night ahead of us and once this air conditioning cuts out it could get very hot in here." As I open the bottle I suddenly realise that we are here for the night. Stephen is right about the heat. It has been a very hot day and without the air conditioning the room could get very hot indeed.

Chapter 36

Looking at me in amusement Stephen laughs suddenly saying, "You never cease to surprise me Bella. Anyone else would be kicking and screaming to get out of here, but not you. You have a lot of guts and I admire you for it." Looking steadily at him I say, "Well maybe now would be a good time to enlighten me before I do just that."
Nodding Stephen sits back in his chair. "As you know I had to visit my brother with the evidence of our affair." As he says it he smiles sexily at me and then laughs as he sees my indignant expression. "Well the fact is I hate my brother and wouldn't help him out in any way at all if it wasn't for Vanessa." His expression softens and he says, "You may be shocked to hear this Bella but Vanessa is not my girlfriend she is my client." I already know all of this but can't reveal it to him as I don't want to blow Ben's cover so I try to look shocked. He looks sadly at me saying, "I didn't have an easy upbringing and so the first opportunity I got I moved away. I cut off all ties with my family and carved a life out for myself away from them. All I had was my looks and sparkling personality." I know that he is trying to make it light hearted but I feel a pang of sympathy for the man in

front of me who has obviously found things tough. Carrying on he says, "I joined an escort agency that caters for high profile customers. They seemed to like me and I learned a lot from them. They weren't so different to me really, in their own way they were also dealt a rough hand and were as emotionally screwed as I was. I take great pleasure in making them happy. It makes me feel valued and as if I am making a difference to them. Many have cheating husbands and I give them their pride back. Most of them just need an attentive escort for the night or for somebody to pay them some attention. Vanessa is one of my regulars. Over this last year we have become quite fond of each other and I find her to be the most kind hearted person that I have ever met. She too hasn't had an easy time of it so we just sort of clicked. Vanessa knew that I had an interest in computers and paid for me to study them in detail in my spare time. It appears that I am a quick learner and have developed quite a flair for them." He stops to take a sip of water and I feel riveted by what he is telling me. I haven't asked him to tell me any of this and I admire him for his honesty. I smile at him to put him at ease. I don't judge him for his career path, if anything I respect him for what he has done. Staring at me once again he says, "When my brother told me of your supposed dealings with his new best friend I had to help Vanessa out. I knew that she had a close personal interest in the stores and counts Ben as one of her closest friends. I was put here to find out what was going on and to expose you at the same time. Vanessa wanted Ben to see you as she thought you were and recover the missing money." As I listen to what he has to say I ask, "Have you found anything out yet?" Stephen smiles thinly saying, "All I have discovered is that you are obviously not involved in anything and are indeed totally in love with your boyfriend. I also know that the money is still going missing and that it is imperative to find out where it is going." Thoughtfully I say, "When you went to see your brother, what did he say when you showed him the evidence?" Stephen frowns and looking annoyed says, "I showed him the photographs and told him that you and Ben had split up. I asked him what would happen when Nathan found out and he just grinned arrogantly and said that he would be pleased that our plan had worked and that he would look forward to moving on to the next stage of his plan. When I asked what that was he just laughed and said that whilst you slept the magic would happen and soon there would be enough evidence to put you in prison and get him released. As soon as he was out he would deposit a hefty sum into my brother's bank account as his share, which he would then split with me." I am now feeling extremely worried. This is all above me and I feel like a puppet being controlled by a maniac. In alarm I say, "What if his plan succeeds? I could go to prison for something I didn't do and Nathan could be free and ruin Ben and Vanessa in the bargain." Stephen's eyes narrow and he says, "That is why we are here Bella. We won't let them succeed; I have a feeling that it is all linked to your computer." Seeing my eyes widen he continues. "During my investigations everything came back to your computer. Anything out of the ordinary came back here and yet still I can't find out what it is." Gesturing to his computers he explains. "These computers are now hooked up to yours and April's. Mikey told me that the magic happens when you slept so I figured that whatever programme that Nathan is running happens during the night. These computers will run concurrently with yours and any information will be passed to them and deciphered. If it is as I think then we should know something by the morning. I look at him in shock. "Do you mean that we have to stay here all night?" Stephen looks at me with a devilish glint in his eyes. "Yes Bella, we do. The alarm is now on and the store locked. We cannot leave this room until the morning. I watched the security guards routine. He always follows the same one. The store is checked methodically after everyone has left. The CCTV is studied and then when they are sure that everyone has left they lock up and go home." In alarm I say, "But won't they have seen us on the CCTV." Stephen looks pleased with himself and says, "I recorded the office earlier after you had left and have linked the recording to the camera on repeat. All they can see is an empty office. They probably just think that you locked it for a reason. You may be asked tomorrow but I doubt it." Looking at Stephen I am amazed at what he can do. "You are pretty amazing yourself Stephen, judging by everything you have told me this evening." Throwing me a look that would bring many grown women to their knees he says, "Takes one to know one Bella. You know you are so lucky to have found Ben. What you two have is special. Not many people have what you have and you should never forget that." My thoughts turn to Ben and I do feel so lucky to have found him again. He is my world and the thought that he wouldn't be in it at all if it hadn't been for Nathan fills me with dread. Seeing Stephen looking at me with a wistful expression I say gently. "You know Stephen, you will find love, probably when you least expect it. You have a lot to give the right person so don't give up on it." Stephen looks at me, a faraway look in his eyes. "I hope that you are right Bella. It's all any of us want really. That is to find that special person that completes you. It is hard to do and people like me look on people like you with jealousy. If I could find someone to share my life with I would be the happiest man alive. Maybe that is what draws me to you Bella. You represent everything that I am looking for. If you weren't already taken let me tell you now, you wouldn't stand a chance against me." I laugh out loud and say cheekily, "There he is, the Stephen that I know. You are so sure of yourself aren't you?" Stephen laughs good naturedly and then grabbing hold of his rucksack he says, "It's going to be a long night Bella. Here, I've brought us some food to keep us going. What is your preference, ham and cheese or cheese and pickle?" He then holds out two packs of sandwiches. "Let's just share them Stephen. One of each, and then you can tell me more about your fascinating life."

Chapter 37

Soon a few hours have passed and I have listened as Stephen tells me stories of life as an escort. I in turn have told him about my life with Ben but I have been careful to keep any reference of Ben's other job well hidden. As Stephen predicted the temperature is rising rapidly in the room and I am becoming extremely hot. Noticing my discomfort Stephen says, "Let's sit on the floor Bella. Heat rises so it's probably the coolest place. We will probably have to sleep here so may as well make ourselves comfortable. I follow him and sit with my back against the wall. Turning to face me Stephen says, "Sorry Bella, do you mind if I take my shirt and trousers off?" Seeing my expression he laughs. "Don't worry; you're perfectly safe I'm just so dammed hot." Fanning myself I reply, "Go ahead, it wouldn't be the first time we have shared the night together after all." Grinning broadly he proceeds to remove his clothing just leaving his boxers on for modesty's sake. If it isn't hot enough in here the temperature is now through the roof. I try not to look at his amazing physique. I thought that Ben had an amazing body but Stephen's is like something out of a magazine. It is toned to perfection and he has more muscles than I have ever seen in my life. He also has some intricate tattoos that surprise me. Seeing me looking at them he sits down beside me and points to one close to his heart. "This one Bella is the first tattoo that I ever had done. It means freedom in Latin. I left home and went straight to get it done. Every day it reminds me of what I left behind and what I want. Fighting the urge to touch it I raise my eyes to his and say softly, "It's beautiful Stephen. Normally I don't like tattoos but they suit you and the fact that they mean something makes them all the more special." He closes his eyes and leans back his head against the wall. A deep sigh comes from within him and I notice that his hand balls into a fist beside him. Then his eyes snap open and he looks wearily at me. "I am not sure that I should have asked you here Bella. I was worried that I would need your help with your passwords and login details but I could probably have coped. It's not fair of me to have involved you." Reaching out I touch his arm and it is like a rod of steel. I notice that he flinches beneath my touch and he groans saying, "Please Bella, I don't think that I can bear it if you touch me. This is unfamiliar territory for me. I have never had to fight to resist someone as much as I am doing with you. Knowing that you are off limits is just adding to the attraction." I quickly shift sideways away from him as I don't want to encourage him in any way. Perhaps he is right I shouldn't have come.

Again the time drags and the room heats up even more. Stephen has closed his eyes and thinking that he is asleep I decide to remove my dress in a faint attempt to get cooler. Luckily I am wearing a full length slip underneath which preserves my modesty. Sipping some more water which is now luke warm I look at the computers. Like Stephen they appear to be asleep. Closing my eyes I wonder what Ben is doing now. I hope that we do find something and then everything can get back to normal.

Soon sleep takes over me. My dreams take me to a dark place. Images of Nathan mixed with Stephen haunt me. I am in a dark forest and they are two animals hunting me. I run deeper and deeper in the forest but they pursue me. I am forced to climb a tree to escape them and they circle at the bottom, calling me to come down. Waking up with a start I realise that it is not them calling me but the gentle tones of Stephen calling my name. In alarm I realise that I have fallen against Stephen and his arm is around me, holding me securely as I sleep against him. Whispering he says, "Bella, wake up, I think I've heard something."

Before I can react though the door is kicked open and in amazement I watch as Ben flies into the room looking angrier than I have ever seen him look before. With a howl of rage he races over and drags Stephen up landing a terrific punch on him. It all happens so quickly and soon they are locked in an almighty fight. They spill out into the corridor and screaming I rush out to try and stop them. Before I can get out of the room though an arm reaches out and blocks my exit. In surprise I see Pete standing in the doorway preventing me from leaving, a worried look on his face. I can only watch helplessly as Ben and Stephen are locked in combat each one landing heavy blows on the other. I struggle to get out, calling for them to stop but Pete looks at me determinedly shaking his head and keeping me from getting involved. Suddenly I notice his eyes widen as he looks behind me into the room and spinning around I see that Stephen's computers have lit up like Christmas Trees. I race back into the room calling Stephen and Ben. "Stephen, Ben quickly, something's happening." Pete also calls them and follows me inside the room. Before I can get there Stephen tears inside closely followed by Ben and we all stand there watching the screens.

"What is it?" I say breathlessly, instantly forgetting everything else, my attention focused on the screen. Stephen says excitedly, "It's working. They are transferring the activity. I'm not sure yet what it all means but the software should soon decipher it and we should know what is happening." Pete shares a look with Ben and Ben says, "What exactly are you doing

Stephen?" Before he can answer Pete says, "It would appear that whatever is happening on Bella's computer is transferring to Stephen's. I would hazard a guess that you have used some sort of decoding software. But how did you know that it was coming from here Stephen?" As I look at Pete I can tell that he is impressed and Stephen says, "I knew that all of the suspect activity came from Bella's computer. After my visit with my brother he told me that it all happens whilst Bella sleeps. It's just a hunch but I needed to see for myself if there was anything happening at night." Looking thoughtful Pete says, "And what were you going to do with this information Stephen when you had it?" Stephen flushes and says, "I was going to hand it over to Vanessa. It would be proof that Bella wasn't involved and she could then hand my findings to the Police and retrieve the stolen money and prove a link to Nathan." Looking angrily at Ben he says, "I know how it looks but I have Bella's best interests at heart. I would never hurt her or you and this was the only way that I could prove her innocence. Also if you hadn't already noticed, it's like an oven in here which should explain our lack of clothing." Looking at Ben I can tell that he is still annoyed but he says, "I'm sorry that I hit you Stephen." Walking over to me he draws me close and says, "I noticed some missed calls and texts from Bella. When I couldn't reach her I was worried and tracked her phone. It appeared to be in your office but there was no reply from there either. I called the security guard at home to ask him if he knew anything, but he said that the store was empty. He did mention though that Bella's office was locked, which was the only unusual thing, however the CCTV showed that it was empty. With Pete's help we realised what you had done Stephen and the rest you know." As I look at Ben and Pete I can see that they are looking at Stephen with some admiration. Squeezing Ben's hand I say, "You should be thanking Stephen. He has gone to a lot of trouble to help prove my innocence. He didn't have to and doesn't deserve the way he has been treated." Shaking his head Stephen says, "It's ok Bella. I would have done the same if I had seen my girlfriend semi naked in someone else's arms. Explanations would have to have waited." Clearing his throat Ben says, "Even so, I am sorry Stephen. I'm afraid it was one time too many and I sort of lost it." Before they can say anything else the computers fall silent again. Seeing their confused looks I say, "What's happening, is that it, have they finished?" Shrugging Stephen says, "Possibly but we won't know for sure until the morning. They may run again later on." Turning to Pete Ben says, "Look Pete, I'm taking Bella home. There's no point in us all being here. The temperature is unbearable. Can I leave this with you?" Nodding Pete says, "Of course, I'll let you know what we find." Then turning to Stephen Ben says, "Once again I am sorry Stephen. Thank you for what you're doing, I really mean that. If there's anything you need just ask and I'll get it." Then he places an arm around my waist and says gently, "Come on Bella, lets get you home." Before we leave I look at Stephen and smile warmly. "Thanks Stephen. Despite what you may or not find I am extremely grateful to you. I am sorry that you got hurt in the process." Grinning ruefully at me Stephen raises his hand and touches his eye which is developing an almighty bruise. "Don't worry Bella, it will all be worth it if we can prove that Nathan is responsible not you and that the money is returned." Ben helps me with my dress and then I follow him out of the room. I hope with all of my heart that things work out for Stephen. I saw another side of him tonight, a vulnerable side that brought out the protector in me. I realise to myself that it must be the same for Vanessa and Ben. I don't think of Stephen in the same way that I do Ben but I would also do anything to protect him. Finally I understand the relationship that Ben and Vanessa share.

Chapter 38

Ben and I don't talk much on the way home. I am just glad that he is here and I soon nod off in the car. Before long we are home and Ben gently shakes me awake. "Come on sleeping beauty, let's get you inside." Leaning against him I wearily head off to bed. The night's events are well and truly catching up with me and all I want now is some sleep.
Once we are in bed Ben pulls me against him and I feel secure feeling his familiar body holding me safe. He whispers, "I love you Bella, you are everything to me and I will do whatever it takes to protect you." Smiling into his chest I say, "I know and it's the same for me too." Soon we drift off to sleep just happy to be together once again.

When I wake up I notice that it must be fairly late as the sun is streaming through the cracks in the curtains and it is already extremely hot. Reaching out for Ben I am not surprised to find his space empty. Before I can do anything else he appears from the bathroom, obviously just having showered. He comes and sits on the bed, a towel slung around his hips, his body still housing the droplets of water from the shower. Reaching over he brushes the hair from my eyes and plants a loving kiss gently on my lips. "Morning Bella, how do you feel?" Reaching up I trace the bruises that have developed on his face. I also notice a cut above one eye and in concern I touch it, noticing that he winces as I do so. In alarm I say, "You're hurt Ben, let me get you something for it." Grabbing my hands in his he pushes me back against the pillows. "Everything I need is here Bella. All I want is to show you how much I love you." Feeling the all too familiar excitement course through me I say, "Let me shower first Ben. I must look a right mess and I feel so hot and sticky." Grinning wickedly at me Ben says, "Just how I like you Bella." Pulling me up against him he runs his fingers through my hair and then pulls me towards him roughly. "Come on, I'll wash you myself. Nothing would give me greater pleasure." Sweeping me up into his arms he carries me squealing to the shower. As the icy cold water hits me I shriek and the reaction makes me move closer into him. Laughing he pushes me against the shower wall and taking the soap proceeds to move it up and down my body, planting kisses as he goes. Soon my body adjusts to the ice cold water and the feeling of the cold water against the heat from inside me that is building the more he touches me sends me over the edge. Grabbing hold of me Ben kisses me passionately his other hand moving up and down my body. The water cascades around us and before I know what is happening Ben carries me from the shower still dripping wet and lays me on the bed. He then proceeds to make love to me and the feeling of the sun hitting my naked body, turning the droplets of water to steam and the excitement that Ben is building in me, drives me insane.

Afterwards we lay our bodies entwined, basking in the sun's rays as they hit our naked bodies. Ben gently strokes my back and once again I fall asleep. When I wake up I am alone again and grabbing my robe I set off to find him.

I see that he is in the kitchen, sitting up at the table with his laptop open as he drinks a coffee. As he sees me enter he smiles sexily saying, "You look amazing Bella. I like the effect I have on you. You look so beautiful." Walking over to him I sit on his lap and wrap my arms around him, pulling him close. "You make me feel beautiful Ben, I love you, have I told you that lately?" Planting a soft kiss on the top of my head he says gently, "I know you do, but I love you more." Mumbling into his chest I say, "That's not possible." I enjoy feeling him against me. I can hear his heart thumping and I inhale his musky scent. I could sit here all day but the phone rings interrupting us.

Leaning over me Ben answers it and just listens as the person at the other end speaks. Looking up at his face his expression gives nothing away and after a brief conversation he hangs up. Moving off of his lap I sit in the chair next to him. "Who was it?" I say looking at him warily. He looks a little relieved and says, "That was Pete. They have discovered where the money is going to but have no proof that Nathan is involved. Apparently the account is in your name Bella, as we thought." He must see the worry in my face because he says, "Don't worry, we all know that it isn't your account. We have to meet the others later where we will find out what the next step will be. It's only a matter of time before we link it to Nathan, we will just have to be patient for a little while longer." His words do not help and all I can think of is the fact that I am still the one with the most at stake. "That's easy for you to say." I say gloomily. Ben reaches over and pulls me towards him. "It affects me as much as you Bella, if not more. I feel powerless at the moment and all I want to do is to make it go away. But rest assured I will stop at nothing to prove that Nathan is behind it, you have my word on that." I don't doubt him for a second but I wonder if this time he has met his match.

Chapter 39

Once again we are back in London sitting in the clinical MI5 meeting room. Once we were ready Ben and I drove here straight away. I feel full of nerves and the worry is well and truly setting in now. All I can think of is that Nathan will succeed in his plan and I could go to prison for something I didn't do. Ben has assured me that this will never happen but I can't shake off the feeling of dread that is gripping me inside.
This time however we are not alone. I am surprised to see Stephen also present. As we walk in he stands up to greet us both looking anxious. I feel Ben stiffen beside me and I greet him warmly, hoping that Ben won't cause another scene.
Before we can speak though Ben's boss breezes into the room followed as always by Pete. I have often wondered about his exact role in the organisation and I vow to ask Ben about it later. Ben's boss looks around the room at us and then says in her crisp authoritative voice, "Sit down everyone, it's good to see you all." Turning to Stephen she says, "Thank you for coming Joseph, it will all become clear to you soon, however once again I must stress how important it is that you do not speak of

anything you hear today to anyone outside of this room. Do I make myself clear?" Stephen, or should I now say Joseph nods meekly and we all take our seats.
As always she gets straight to it and says, "Well we have now discovered the whereabouts of the stolen money. It is currently residing in an off shore bank account in Bella's name. The problem now is to link it to Nathan and clear Bella of any involvement. You will be pleased to know that we have formulated a plan and with any luck it may just succeed." She then turns to Pete and says, "Show her in." I look at Ben to see if he knows what's going on but he just shrugs and looks with interest at the door. I can feel the tension in the room and we all sit in silence waiting for Pete to come back with the mystery guest. We don't have long to wait and it is with considerable surprise and shock that we all watch as Pete holds open the door and in walks Melissa. The fact that she is here is not the shock, it is how she looks. Gone is the self assured model type that could beguile any man in her path. This Melissa is in a terrible state. Her arm is in plaster and she has the biggest bruise on her face and arms. She is limping and I notice a bandage covering her right knee. Her mouth is bruised and swollen and there is a nasty cut above her right eye. Tears spring to my eyes at how fragile she has become and to say I am shocked is an understatement. Ben

smiles at her sweetly and pulls out a chair for her. I notice that he doesn't look surprised at her appearance though. Joseph is looking as shocked as me although this is his first meeting with Melissa I am sure. Looking around at us all she smiles softly and says, "Hi Ben, Bella, it's good to see you both." Her eyes turn to Joseph and she says, "I am pleased to meet you Joseph. I have heard good things about you." Joseph looks at her in surprise and I can tell that he is lost for words. That will be a first I think with some amusement. Ben's boss then speaks up saying, "Thanks for coming Melissa. I am sorry to drag you in here away from your recuperation but as you know we could do with your help." Looking around at us all she adds, "For your information Melissa has just been involved in a horrific car accident. That is all I am going to say on the matter and it has absolutely no bearing on our operation. Despite the fact that she should be resting Melissa has agreed to help us, as we believe that she is the only one who can. Right then here it is." Turning to Joseph she says, "You must go to see your brother and tell him that you have discovered the whereabouts of Melissa. As we know this is the information that Nathan most wants and he will do anything for it. You must tell your brother that if Nathan sends her a visiting order you will accompany her to see him. But it will come at a price. He must transfer

£20,000 into your account before you both arrive and then a further £20,000 when you have left. This we hope will be the proof that Nathan controls the account. I have briefed Melissa on what she needs to do but Joseph must make his brother believe that she works for the same escort agency that he does. This information will drive Nathan mad; however once he sees her all hell is sure to break loose. Ben and Bella, I brought you here to keep you informed of what is going on. There is nothing that you can do but to carry on the pretence that you have split up. I am confident that this won't take long to resolve if everyone stays in character and plays their part. Now I must go but Pete has all the details and he will brief you individually. Thank you for coming and good luck."

She stands up abruptly and leaves the room. I notice that Melissa looks uncomfortable and wonder what injuries she sustained. I cannot help but feel very sorry for her. She has always been so poised and self assured and sitting here she looks vulnerable and somewhat broken. I also notice that Stephen appears mesmerised by her. He can't take his eyes off of her and I remember how kind hearted he is and the sight of her sitting here so damaged will have brought out the protector in him.

Pete looks around and then passes a large brown envelope to both Joseph and Melissa. "Here are your instructions with everything that you need. Keep in touch with each other and as soon as the visiting order comes through we can put the plan into action." Looking with compassion at Melissa, Pete says, "Are you sure you're up to this Mel? If you're not we can sort something else out." Melissa shakes her head and I see some of the old fire in her eyes. "I wouldn't miss it for the world Pete. By the time I have finished with him Nathan Matthews won't know what hit him." Smiling to myself I am glad to see that the old Melissa is still in there. Pete says, "Ok, if you're sure. Ben, Melissa we just need a quick word. Joseph, Bella if you wouldn't mind waiting there's a coffee shop downstairs. Ben won't be long and he can drop you both home. I'll be in touch soon." Ben looks at me and raises his eyes. He doesn't look happy and I know it's because he doesn't want to leave me with Joseph. I smile reassuringly at him as he leaves with the others.

As they leave Joseph lets out his breath. "Well that was intense. I can't believe any of this." He gestures around at the room and I laugh saying, "I must admit it took me by surprise at first. How did you find out?" Joseph grins and says, "When you left last night Pete and I carried on. The computers started up again three more times and the more that Pete and I talked I realised that his knowledge went beyond that of a paid employee of Ben's. I didn't say anything though and just before we left he took a call. He asked me to go with him to discuss our findings and before I knew what was happening he brought me here. The lady that came in with him earlier met us and told me about their real occupations. I had to swear that I wouldn't talk about it otherwise it would jeopardise everything." In surprise I say, "So you haven't even slept?" Looking weary Stephen says, "No, but I don't think that I could if I tried. This is way more exciting than sleep." Laughing I say, "Come on then, you obviously are in dire need of a coffee. My treat for all of your help."

We find a corner in the coffee shop and sink back against the padded seats. I can see Joseph's eyes shining with excitement and say, "I can't get used to hearing you called Joseph. I still think of you as Stephen." Looking slightly embarrassed he says, "You should try having two names. I don't know who I am half the time. I suppose that when this is over Stephen will be out of a job. The real Stephen will be back soon and may discover that there is somebody with his name and Id masquerading as a store manager." He laughs but I can tell that he is subdued at the thought. With interest I say, "So what next. Will you carry on in your previous job?" He takes a sip of his coffee and looks thoughtful. "I

expect so. Although I am going to carry on with the computer side of things. I may start my own business and just carry on with my other job on the side."
I sit silently thinking of his predicament. I know that he loves his escort work and I wouldn't judge him on it for a second as he obviously takes a lot of pride in it. However I know that all he really wants is to settle down and I wonder if he could find someone doing what he does. Smiling over he says, "Penny for them.." Laughing awkwardly I say, "I hope it all works out for you Joseph. You are a decent man and have a lot to offer. I can't thank you enough for what you did for me and I will always be here for you if you need anything. I really mean that." Joseph smiles sadly. "That means a lot Bella; however I expect that after this our paths won't cross much. Ben will certainly see to that and I don't blame him. I wouldn't like my girlfriend having a friendship with someone who obviously adores her." His words silence me and I blush. Laughing he says, "I wondered where my embarrassed Bella went to. I'm glad to see that I haven't lost my touch." Raising my eyes at him we both laugh and then we hear, "Something funny?" Looking up we see Ben standing beside us looking annoyed. My heart sinks. He is still obviously really put out and I feel bad for Joseph. I look at him and say, "Not really, but any laughter is good after the last

few days events don't you think?" Sliding in beside me Ben looks wearily at us. "Yes, I'm sorry. It's this place." He gestures around us. "There aren't many laughs to be had here let me tell you. Anyway, I'm to get you home Joseph so that you can get some sleep. Then I must take you home Bella and then return to London. Let's just hope this doesn't take too long and we can all return to normal." Hearing his words my heart sinks. He's leaving again. Reaching for his hand I give it a squeeze and he looks at me sadly. "Don't worry Bella, it will soon be over." Leaning over he kisses my forehead distractedly and I can feel Joseph's eyes staring at me from across the table. I don't look at him because I don't want to see his expression. Inwardly I pray that he meets someone soon, he is a lost soul and deserves happiness.

Chapter 40

As promised we drop Stephen home and soon find ourselves once again saying goodbye as Ben leaves for London. Drawing me close to him Ben kisses me passionately and I can feel the desperation in him. Smoothing my hair away from my face he says, "I love you Bella. Stay strong and I will be back soon." Reaching up I trace the contours of his face and place a gentle kiss on his lips. "I love you too Ben. Don't worry about anything; let's just hope that this is over soon." He pulls away and once again I feel my heart ache as I watch him drive off. Almost as soon as he is out of sight I hear the phone ringing and wearily go inside to answer it. "Bella, thank goodness. I have been calling you all day." My heart lifting I say, "Phoeb's I'm glad it's you, how are you?" I can tell something's up as she says shortly, "Never mind all that I'm coming round and you had better start talking. I'll be 15 minutes." She hangs up abruptly and I realise that she must have heard something about Ben and I. This is going to be awkward. True to her word Phoebe is soon knocking on the door and as I let her in she flings her arms around me and hugs me tightly. "I can't believe that I have just heard that you and Ben are having problems." She draws back and I feel guilty as I see the hurt in her eyes. My expression sombre I say, "I can't really explain it all Phoebe as it's complicated. Who told you?" Following me inside she sits down heavily on the settee in the kitchen. "Your mum rang and asked if I had seen you as she hadn't heard from you and was worried. She filled me in and was surprised that I didn't know. Why didn't you tell me B, I always thought that we told each other everything?" Now I feel extremely guilty and realise that I have been so wrapped up in my own misery that I should have told her that something was wrong. Sitting next to her I say, "I'm sorry Phoebs. I just hoped that it would all be resolved before I had to involve you in my mess. You must be fed up with my constant problems with Ben and I suppose I didn't want to drag it all up." Phoebe's eyes narrow and I remember that she knows me too well and nothing gets past her. I blush and look down and I can feel her staring at me. Then she says, "Boris told me that Ben has been seeing that other woman again. Is it true?" Fiddling nervously with my hands I nod miserably. Carrying on she says, "And your mum told me that there was another man interested in you, your new boss?" Again I nod but can't seem to look at her. Sighing Phoebe says, "Right then I will make us both a drink and you can tell me everything. I am not

leaving until you have. I don't care if you are having a torrid affair with this man but I want to help you and you can't bottle it all up."
Standing up she proceeds to make us both a drink, giving me some time to gather my thoughts. I hate lying to her but I know that I must. There's too much at stake and I must stick to the plan. This had all better be over soon before I lose all of my friends in the bargain.
For the next few hours I try to convince Phoebe that the story I tell is a true one. She isn't my best friend for nothing though and I know that she hasn't bought any of it. She stays for most of the day but before she leaves she fixes me with an unwavering stare saying, "I haven't believed anything Bella but I know that you have your reasons. When you are ready to tell me the true story I will be here. In the meantime I hope that whatever it is resolves itself quickly for both your sakes and then maybe you can finally tell me what on earth is going on." Leaning over she kisses me on the cheek and hugs me warmly. "Don't worry I know that you must be going through something major. Just remember that I am always here for you day or night and would never betray your confidence. Come and stay with us if you want and I promise not to dig any further." Tears spring into my eyes and I will myself not to crumble. More than anything I want to tell her everything right here and now

but I have come so far I can't risk it. Squeezing her tightly I say, "I promise you Phoebs. As soon as I can I will tell you everything. I love you so much, you know that don't you?" Nodding she hugs me again and we stand there for some time just hugging each other, both of us unwilling to let go.
When Phoebe finally leaves I drag myself off to bed. I need a lot of sleep to catch up and hope that when I wake up I will feel more able to cope with everything.

For the next few days I throw myself into my job. I am sure that April knows that something is up as I catch her giving me many puzzled looks. I just carry on and work long hours just to distract me from my situation. I do still speak to Ben every night and he is also finding things hard. It's the waiting that is unbearable and I wonder how long it will be. I don't see Joseph around the store which is lucky as I may slip up and call him by his real name. I do hear that he is on leave which in some ways makes me relax but strangely I also miss seeing him.
It must be a week later when Ben rings me at about 7am and I can hear the excitement in his voice. "Bella, get ready we have been told to report to HQ this morning. I'll come and get you." I feel excited and say, "Why, what's happening?" He laughs saying, "All will be revealed. Be ready in an hour, we'll know more later."

As I get ready a knot forms in my stomach. I hope that it is good news. I almost daren't hope that Ben can return home with me later, it almost seems impossible.
As soon as he arrives I launch myself at him. Every time I see him I just want to feel him close to me. Clinging on to him I savour the feel of him against me and breathe in his heavenly scent. Laughing he pulls back and kisses me gently. He says huskily, "Careful Bella, I'm on a short enough fuse as it is. Unfortunately we haven't got much time otherwise I would show you just how much I have missed you." Looking at him seductively I say, "Why don't you then, they can wait can't they?" Looking tortured Ben groans saying, "If only they could. I am afraid I have strict instructions to get there on time and with the rush hour traffic that may prove impossible. We have to leave now." Disappointed I follow him to the car. However I make sure that I tease him all the way by running my hand up and down his leg and applying pressure where he needs it the most. It doesn't take long before he grabs my hand firmly and places it in my lap. "Behave yourself Bella before I have more than one accident." Laughing I move away but then images of Melissa and her damaged body spring to mind and I instantly feel bad. "Ben, what happened to Melissa?" I say, not really expecting him to tell me. I know that none of them give much away but I am curious. Sighing

heavily he says grimly, "She was in a bad car accident that much is true. However not all of her injuries came from it. Things went badly wrong with her operation and she took quite a beating. Before the back up could go in to assist her she was dragged into a car and there was a hell of a chase. The consequences were that there was a terrible crash and she was thrown from the car. The car fell down a steep embankment and burst into flames, killing the other occupants. She was taken to hospital and had to endure an emergency operation to save her life. She is lucky to be alive and I have never seen her as shaken up as she was and still is to some extent. I just hope that she gets some time to readjust but she is in so much demand as she is one of our best operatives."
Sinking back in my seat I am in shock. Once again I am reminded of the dangerous job that they do and I pray that Ben can get out soon.

We travel the rest of the way in silence. Ben's story has brought it all home and I realise how serious the situation is. It doesn't take long and we are soon pulling in to the car park beneath the MI5 building.

Ben signs me in again and I am surprised when he doesn't lead me to our usual lift. Instead he crosses the reception area to the opposite side and presses the lift to go down. Looking at him in surprise he just smiles saying, "Different venue today Bella. Your wish is about to come true." I can feel the excitement building within me. Finally I am going to see the real workings of this operation.

Chapter 41

Ben takes me down another long corridor to a room situated at the end. He enters a pass code and we find ourselves in an empty room with another locked door at the end. I notice cameras placed strategically around the room and I see them moving with red lights flickering inside them. Ben punches another code in and we find ourselves in another room where there are shelves housing plastic trays. Turning to me Ben says, "Put your bag and anything in your pockets in that tray Bella." I watch as he empties his pockets and puts his phone, keys, wallet and belt into the tray. Winking at me he says, "Just like at the airport." I do as he says and then we proceed through another coded door. Putting his hand up to prevent me following him straight away he says, "One at a time Bella; me first and then you." Looking up I can see that the door is different and realise that it is scanning us like they do at the airport. Now I know why Ben can't be contacted most of the time that he is here. Once we have gone through I follow him silently down another long corridor. I feel quite overwhelmed and nervous. Seeing my expression Ben takes my hand and gives it a gentle squeeze. "It's ok Bella, don't worry. Your bag will be safe where it is. The room is under constant surveillance and to my knowledge nothing has ever been stolen from there." I actually hadn't given that much thought. I am more intimidated by the thought of what I might find at the end of this journey.

Ben stops outside a large door and once again punches in a code. As the door opens I am amazed to see that we are in a large room that appears to be some sort of control room. There are rows and rows of screens and computers and many people sitting in front of them apparently monitoring things and looking at the information in front of them. Nobody looks up and just carries on with what they are doing. Suddenly I spot a familiar face as Pete approaches us smiling. "Bella, good to see you. Welcome to our home." He laughs and I smile nervously back at him. Then his boss approaches from another room and says, "Right then everything is in place, I'll show you where you'll sit." I look at Ben in surprise and he winks reassuringly at me. I almost wonder if I am to be interrogated; maybe they are going to test my innocence by hooking me up to a lie detector or something. However all that happens is that Ben's boss shows us to a row of monitors and gestures for us to sit down. She says briskly, "Joseph and Melissa are in place and the fun is just about to start. We brought you here Bella as this concerns you more than anyone. You can see what happens when Melissa visits Nathan and let us know if there is anything that is said that seems strange." I almost laugh as everything about this day is strange but I keep my thoughts to myself and just nod in agreement. As they take their places beside me they hand me a set of headphones. Placing them on my head they all do the same and we sit silently looking at the screens. I stare at the image in front of me in fascination. I can see that we are looking at what appears to be a prison. There is a big room with tables and chairs set out and I watch as what appears to be the prisoners are being led in. They all take their seats and then I see him. I am shocked as I see the unmistakeable figure of Nathan, approaching his seat, scanning the room anxiously. My heart beats faster and faster as I look at him. He has lost weight and looks pale and anxious. His hair is very short and I can tell that he is nervous. All of his confidence appears to have deserted him and he looks a shadow of his former self. I watch as he plays with his hands, throwing anxious looks towards the door. All of a sudden the doors open and the visitors swarm in. I see Joseph enter and watch with interest as he approaches a man who I immediately see is his brother. They do look similar although his brother is not a patch on Joseph. Then I see Nathan's eyes widen in shock as Melissa enters the room. She approaches his table slowly and obviously in considerable discomfort. Nathan jumps up in alarm and goes towards her but a prison guard immediately pushes him back down into his seat. It appears that Nathan isn't the only one watching her. All eyes are on her as she crosses the room. Even in her bruised and battered state she is a vision. It wouldn't surprise me if she caused a prison riot such is the fascination on the faces of the inmates. I watch with interest as she sits down awkwardly in front of him. Even from here I can see every expression on their faces. Her lip trembles as she looks at him and her eyes fill with tears. Nathan looks devastated and his eyes also fill with tears. Then to my surprise the sound comes on and we can hear them speak. Nathan says in a husky voice filled with emotion. "Melissa, baby, what have they done to you?" Melissa lowers her eyes and replies breathlessly, "I've missed you so much Nathan. As you can see, life hasn't been good for me since you were arrested either." Nathan reaches out and grabs her hands and his voice breaking he says, "Who did this to you; please tell me I want to know?" Once again Melissa's lip trembles and in a small voice she says, "Don't judge me Nathan but I had to make a living. You were gone and I couldn't go back to my old job. The only option open to me was to work as an escort." Tears spill down her face and Nathan looks devastated. Tears run down his face and he says, "Did somebody do this to you?" Melissa nods and wipes her eyes. She speaks softly and falteringly saying, "I tried to get away but they wouldn't let me." Nathan's head snaps up and he says, "They?" Melissa weeps uncontrollably and says, "There was a party. I escorted a new client and it all seemed ok at first. Then as the evening went on he became more invasive and started to demand more of me than I wanted to give. I tried to tell him that I wasn't that kind of escort but he wasn't having any of it." She stops and gulps and then raises her eyes to his and I can see the hurt and pain that she directs towards him. Nathan's eyes narrow menacingly and he says, "What happened next?" Lowering her eyes Melissa says in a whisper. "He pulled me into a room but we were not alone. There were several other couples in there and.." She breaks off sobbing uncontrollably and Nathan balls his fists in anger and says, "What happened Melissa, I mean it I have to know." Looking directly at him tears coursing down her face she says, "They raped me Nathan. Not just him but several of them. They beat me and I was lucky to get out of there alive. So now you know. I had nobody to protect me and I don't know what I am going to do." My breath catches in my throat as I watch Nathan's reaction. He is like a caged animal and I remember being the one on the end of his anger the last time I saw him and it wasn't a pleasant experience. If he wasn't in prison there would be no stopping him. I notice that Joseph and his brother are also watching the drama intently and I feel riveted to the screen. The prison guard sensing the threat approaches the table but Nathan just says, "Its ok, we're fine." The guard steps back but keeps his eye on them. Leaning over Nathan grabs Melissa's hands. "Don't worry Baby, I will look after you." Melissa looks at him in confusion saying, "But how can you, you are locked away in here. I have nobody Nathan. Look at me; I can't even get a job as an escort looking like this. I am finished." Angrily Nathan says, "You are never going back there, that much is certain. I may be incarcerated but I still have control over certain things." Looking at him in bewilderment Melissa says, "What do you mean, control over what?" Leaning towards her he caresses her hands and gazes adoringly at her. "If I have my way I won't be in here for much longer." Looking at him in shock, her baby blue eyes now huge she says in a whisper, "What do you mean?" Nathan smiles wickedly saying, "Just a little insurance policy that's about to mature. Soon there will be proof that I am innocent and somebody else will be taking my place. The people that did this to me will suffer and lose everything whilst I will walk free and claim what's mine." Hearing him speak I feel so angry. The only person that did this to him was himself. How dare he try to harm us in an act of vengeance. Sensing my anger Ben places a hand on mine and squeezes it. He doesn't speak and his attention goes back to the screen. Looking excited Melissa gazes at Nathan, her eyes drawing him in. I can see her rubbing the top of his hand and she runs her tongue over her lips. Nathan's eyes darken and we can hear his breathing quicken. Huskily she says, "Tell me baby, what are you going to do?" Lowering his voice he says, "Get Joey to take you to my parent's house. I will call them and tell them to give you my keys. On the key ring is a key to a safety deposit box at the bank. The number is on it and I will call them to expect your visit. Inside you will find £100,000. Take it and use it to rent somewhere for us. There is also an envelope with it addressed to the Police. Mail it; don't deliver it by hand, and then you watch. There is enough evidence in there to link my crime to another. They will then have no choice but to let me go." He looks very pleased with himself and Melissa smiles sexily at him. "I knew you would be there for me baby." She says, fluttering her large eyelashes at him. I can't wait for you to come out of here, I've missed you, you know you're the only one for me." I can see the torture on his face at the fact that he cannot touch her. She is playing a blinder and I have almost forgotten that she is playing a part. The sexual tension is even travelling into our room as we watch and you could hear a pin drop. Suddenly the bell rings in the prison, making us all jump, signifying that visiting time is over. Nathan looks at Melissa in anguish and she smiles sexily at him saying, "For now baby, we will have all the time in the world soon." She catches his hand and presses it to her heart. She holds his gaze with hers and then a prison guard moves over to break them up. She watches as Nathan is led away, her gaze never leaving him for a second. Then he is gone and we watch as Joseph crosses the room and helps her up. As they walk away her expression is blank.

The screen goes blank and I watch as the three people next to me sit back in their chairs and look at each other. I can see the excitement blazing in their eyes and realise just how much this all means to them. They are all linked, they thrive on it all and I can see the adrenalin pumping through them by way of their expressions. Letting out a deep breath Ben's boss says, "Get well soon Melissa, God I need you." Looking at the others she laughs saying, "I always did call her my weapon of mass destruction. I could watch her at work all day long." The others laugh and I can see why they love their job so much. Looking at them I say, "What happens next?" Pete says, "We wait. It won't take them long to get the key and they will bring the contents of the box back here. Then we will know what we're dealing with." Their Boss says, "Pete, get a team onto them at the bank.

Make sure they aren't disturbed and then get them a car to bring them back here." Pete heads off and she says to us, "You two may as well grab some lunch. I'll text you when they return. Let's just hope that this can be resolved today." She sweeps out of the room leaving Ben and I alone. Looking at him nervously I say, "What if there's something in there that incriminates me. How much influence does your boss have?" Laughing Ben draws me closer to him saying, "That envelope will go nowhere near the Police and even if it does nothing will happen. Nathan won't be released that much I am certain about. They will link this crime to him and his sentence will undoubtedly be extended. Anyway, come on let's get something to eat."

Chapter 42

Ben and I make our way outside and find a nice little café near the river. I am quiet though because I am taking in everything that I have just seen. As I watch Ben sitting opposite me looking out of the window I can see that he is also dwelling on everything. Seeing them all at work today I realise that Ben will never be able to truly give this up. It runs deep within them all and the excitement that I witnessed on all of their faces showed me what it all means to them. They are a family, joined in a common purpose. I feel very much on the outside looking in and wonder just what other experiences they have all shared. Ben may not want to go out in the field again but even I know he won't turn his back on them. Almost as if he knows what I am thinking Ben leans over the table taking my hands in his. "Don't worry Bella. You will be cleared and we can get back to normal soon." Looking fearfully at him I say, "Whatever normal is?" Looking thoughtful he says, "I am not the person I was before I met you Bella. I am not going out in the field again; it's not fair on you. There will still be a role for me though as back up behind the scenes. I can't give it up completely, it's in my blood." Squeezing his hand I smile reassuringly at him. "I know that Ben.

What will your boss do without one of her best operatives though?" Grinning Ben says, "Oh I think that she will soon have a new toy to play with." My eyes widening I say, "Joseph?" Ben nods and we both laugh. Goodness, I wonder what he will say when he has that conversation, I wonder with interest. Thinking of Joseph I realise that he is the perfect replacement for Ben. He has proved that he is loyal and not afraid to go out on a limb for something or someone that he cares about. He is also devastatingly handsome and there won't be many who would be able to resist him. He also has a likeable quality that will help him enormously. All of that coupled with his obvious flair for computers should make him go far. Maybe it will give him a purpose in life and I feel excited for him.

After we have eaten Ben and I go for a walk along the South Bank. We walk our arms around each other and I enjoy the fact that we are together, out in the fresh air and away from the drama that is sure to unfold later on. Our happiness is short lived though as Ben's phone rings, shattering the peace. He doesn't speak and just hangs up and looks at me with a serious expression. "They'll be back soon. We need to join the others." With a mixture of trepidation and excitement I follow him back to the MI5 building.

Once again we follow the same procedure as before and are soon back downstairs, but this time in a different room. This one is smaller, with no windows and just a few seats around a table. There is a coffee machine in the corner and we help ourselves whilst we wait. We don't wait there for long before Ben's boss breezes into the room, closely followed by Pete, Joseph and Melissa. As I look at their expressions I can see excitement blazing in all their faces. They have obviously found something of importance and I am intrigued to find out what it is. Ben's boss gestures for them to take a seat and once they are all placed she says, "Ok Melissa, tell us what you found."

We all look at her expectantly and I notice that Joseph's expression is also one of excitement. Seeing me looking he winks at me and grins. This doesn't go unnoticed by Ben who immediately tenses up next to me. Ignoring the two of them I concentrate on what Melissa has to say. Looking around she says in a blank tone. "I won't go into what was said at the prison as I know that you all saw and heard our conversation. Once we left Joseph drove me to Nathan's parent's house. His mother was expecting us and after a few pleasantries handed us a set of keys. On closer inspection I could tell that there was one security deposit box key present. Promising to return them we left for the bank. It didn't take long and we were soon able to access the box that the key fitted. On opening the box we found the money that Nathan had said was there as well as the envelope." She then pulls the money and the envelope out of her bag and puts them on the table. I can't believe how much money is in front of me and I have to blink to make sure that it is real. Ben's boss leans over and opens the envelope. We all look with interest as a sheaf of documents come out of it followed by a passport and what appears to be a plane ticket. Ben's boss studies them and then directs her gaze to me. "It would appear that this is a list of passwords and account details for an account in your name Bella. The passport is also yours and an open ticket to Switzerland, one way" I can feel them all studying me and I say in confusion. "That can't be my passport. Mine is at home where it's always been. In fact I haven't long used it when we went on holiday. How could Nathan have got it when he is in prison?" Turning to me Ben says gently. "It's obviously a copy. The account is also in your name and he would have used the fake passport to open it and buy the ticket. I would bet that this account is where the money from the store goes. Whether or not it is still there remains to be seen." Ben's boss nods and says, "That we can check, but we still need a link to Nathan." Stephen then speaks up. "The money that he promised my brother has been paid into my account. He obviously has access to another bank account as I am sure that he wouldn't want any connection between Bella and his prison buddies brother. It could then provide the police with the link they need." Looking thoughtful Ben's boss says, "Any ideas?" Smiling Melissa says, "These weren't the only things that we found in the safety deposit box." She then proceeds to take another folder and a small box out of her bag. "In this folder are details of another account. The name on the front is VE which could be somebody's initials or the name of the company. There is also another passport and ticket and several credit cards all in the name of Marcus Butler." Looking at her in amazement I am surprised to see the same cool calm matter of fact expression on her face as she looks around her. Ben's boss looks thoughtful. "It looks as though Nathan had it all planned. Bella was his get out of jail free card and he had a new identity waiting for him. It appears that he thought of everything." Stunned I try to take it all in. Then Ben speaks up. "This other account must have been set up to receive the money that he has stolen. However in setting Bella up her account would be frozen and any money in it seized. There must be something else that we are missing. It could be connected to these initials. Could it be another target that he is also stealing from?" Pete replies, "We will run a check on both accounts and see where they lead us. If there is any money in this account we can trace where it originated from." Stephen then interrupts. "If Nathan is in prison though how can he be controlling the accounts? To my knowledge computer use is strictly monitored in prison so how can he have transferred the money to my account in the first place?" Pete says, "You can get anything in prison for the right price. My guess is that he has a mobile phone hidden and is controlling his bank account from there." Ben's boss says, "Ok, let's order a search and find the phone. We will also track the accounts and try to prove the link. Good job Melissa and you too Joseph. I would suggest that you all return home and let Pete and I organise everything. We will be in touch once we have the answers. In the meantime if anyone thinks of anything let Pete know." Everyone stands up to leave but something is still niggling at me. I am sure that the initials mean something to me and I rack my brains to think where I know them from. Ben looks questioningly at me and says, "What is it Bella, what's bothering you?" Raising my eyes I see them all looking at me curiously and then it comes to me. "The initials VE, I think I know what they mean." They all sit down again and I say, "Nathan is a huge Star Trek fan. It used to drive me mad and he always said that if he ever had his own company he would call it, Vulcan Enterprises. A play on two words from his favourite series, it must be the name of the company that he has set up to receive the stolen money." Ben's boss smiles broadly and turning to me says, "Well done Bella. Pete, search for Vulcan Enterprises and find out everything you can about the company. If Nathan is planning anything at all through this account we should soon know about it. Ok, we have work to do. Joseph, please can you take Melissa home and I will be in touch with you all as soon as I have the information." She goes to leave but then turns back and looks at me saying, "Oh, and Bella, don't worry about any of it. There's enough evidence here to clear your name at least."

She leaves the room closely followed by Pete and as the door shuts Melissa laughs hollowly. "Typical Zo, matter of fact and to the point. How I've missed her dulcet tones." Seeing Ben frown she raises her eyes and says, "What? We all know what she's like; I don't know how Pete puts up with her." Then turning to Joseph she says sweetly, "If it's out of your way I can get a cab home." I notice Joseph looks a bit shell shocked and I feel quite sorry for him. Despite being a huge player himself I am sure that even he is out of his league with Melissa, even in her broken state. I see Ben grinning knowingly and Joseph just shakes his head and says, "I wouldn't hear of it. Here let me help you." Turning to us Melissa smiles and says, "It's been great seeing you both again. I'm glad that I could help out. Nathan Matthews shouldn't bother you again." Mumbling my thanks I watch as Joseph takes her arm carefully and follows her out of the room. Ben grins at me and I raise my eyes up. "He doesn't stand a chance does he?" Ben laughs and grabs hold of me. "Probably not, but one day Melissa will meet her match and I was kind of hoping that it was him. Anyway, I've had enough of this place for one day, let's grab something to eat on our way home and then I have plans for you this evening." All of a sudden I have suddenly lost my appetite and I hope that he chooses fast food.

Chapter 43

Things return to normal for a couple of days at least and it is all I can do to concentrate on my job. Ben had to return to London as we still had to keep up the pretence that we have separated. However seeing that there may be a light at the end of the tunnel doesn't make it as bad this time.

I don't see Joseph at all and wonder if he will ever return to the store. Once this is all over I am sure that he will be otherwise occupied if what Ben says is true.

As I am packing away for the evening at work the door to our office opens and I see April's eyes widen. Turning to see who came in I am pleased to see Ben lounging in the doorway leaning on the door frame and looking sexily at me. I laugh as I see April blush and turning to her he says, "Hi April. Long time no see." She blushes even further and I raise my eyes up. He knows how intimidated she is by him and I laugh inwardly. Jumping up April gathers her things saying, "Pleased to see you again Mr Hardcastle. See you tomorrow Bella, have a good evening."

As soon as she leaves we grin at each other. "So Ben, to what do I owe this lovely surprise?" Moving across the room Ben takes me in his arms. "Unfortunately we have been summoned to London; otherwise I would be tempted to show you just how much I've missed you right here and now." He laughs as he sees my wanton expression. Just the mere thought of it is enough to turn my legs to jelly. He is like a drug to me and I am totally addicted. "Come on Bella, let's get this over with." I follow him outside, wondering what we are going to discover.

We don't speak much on the journey and I sense that Ben is as unsettled as I am. This business has been so personal to us both and I will be relieved when it is over. Soon we have gone through the rigmarole of security and once again find ourselves in the same office as before.
Helping ourselves to a coffee we wait for the others to arrive. We don't have to wait long before Joseph joins us, closely followed by Melissa. I notice that she still looks extremely fragile and Joseph rushes to pull out a seat for her. I smile at him and he grins at me sheepishly. "So Ben, how's my favourite pretend boyfriend?" Melissa says looking flirtatiously at Ben. Ben laughs softly saying, "Happy with my real girlfriend Melissa, how about you, that was a nasty experience you just had?" Joseph is now looking extremely confused and I

try to stop from laughing. Melissa grimaces. "I am not going to lie it wasn't pleasant. But you know me, I'll soon bounce back and once more into the fray I will go." Looking concerned Ben says, "You should take some time out like Tina did. It's not good for you to jump from one job to another. You need some down time." Shrugging she says, "What can I say, I live to work. Nothing gives me greater pleasure and when I am not on an operation my life has no meaning." I feel very sorry for her as I hear her speak and can see a thoughtful expression on Joseph's face. The door suddenly opens and their boss and Pete come into the room. Sitting down she gets straight to business. "We have now traced both accounts. The one in Bella's name shows several transactions amounting to several hundreds of thousands of pounds. The money stays in the account but at certain intervals some of the money has been transferred to another account." Looking at her with interest Ben says, "Which one?" Looking directly at him she says, "Your account Ben." In shock Ben says, "It can't, I would have noticed if there was a large sum of money there." Staring at him with a hard expression she says, "Not your own account but another one in your name." I look at Ben in confusion and he just stares at her with interest. "He is probably linking the two of you to take the blame together. It would appear that Nathan was very busy before his arrest. He has to our knowledge opened 3 new accounts at the bank. One in Bella's name, one in Ben's and one in his new identity Marcus Butler." Ben interrupts saying, "How on earth could he open accounts in our name. Surely he would have to have gone there with ID?" Looking sternly at him she says, "According to the CCTV footage he did just that. He went with a female who looked remarkably like Bella, and they both opened the accounts in Ben and Bella's name. The passports were both forged. Nathan probably had his photo against Ben's name but because he needed it to be Bella's passport that was found in the box he had to have a double pose as her for identification purposes." I see Melissa grinning as she says, "Wow, he really had it in for you two." "That's enough." Snaps their boss. "He probably opened the third one at a later date. Anyway we ran a fingerprint check and luckily the woman's prints were still on the fake passport and we found a match for them on our database." I look at Ben in astonishment as she continues. "Her name is Gina Monroe and has been pulled in several times for petty crimes. It didn't take long for her to spill the beans in return for community service. She is also willing to testify in court against Nathan. This will prove that he set you up Bella so you have no more cause to worry." I feel as if a huge weight has been lifted and slump back in my chair with relief.

Joseph smiles at me and Ben reaches over and grabs my hand, giving it a gentle squeeze. Pete then says, "We also traced the company that Nathan has set up. It is as Bella said called, Vulcan enterprises and it lists Marcus Butler as the owner. Currently it houses funds of £500,000 and there are a few transactions showing recently, the one to Joseph's bank included." Ben's boss adds, "We ordered a search of his cell whilst he was otherwise occupied and have found his phone. We inserted a surveillance device and replaced it. We are currently monitoring the phone and have discovered an interesting link between his bank account and a certain well known bank." Ben and Stephen both look up in alarm and she nods saying, "Yes, Montague's Bank is the intended target. We think that once Nathan is released due to his plan to frame Bella succeeding, he will start the process to raid the bank's coffers overnight. The money will be transferred to his Vulcan account and he will have left the country. The bank will fold along with the stores. By the time the money is traced he will be long gone and the money withdrawn." She sits back and we all sit silently digesting what she has just told us. I knew that Nathan was corrupt but this beggar's belief. I am finding it very hard to remember the man that I had fallen in love with just a few short years ago. Melissa looks thoughtful and breaks the silence. "So what happens now. Do you release him?" Their boss says, "No, it won't come to that. We may need your help though Melissa, one last time on this particular operation with any luck. Your's too Joseph. We can contain this and get our proof without any damage if we play our cards right." Joseph looks intrigued. "Of course I will do anything to help." Their boss nods and says, "Good, then this is the plan. Melissa and Joseph will once again visit the prison. Joseph will tell his brother that Bella has been arrested but there is a press ban due to the sensitive nature regarding the stores. We will also arrange for a solicitor to visit Nathan instructing him that his case has been re opened and he can expect to be released the next day. Melissa, you will go and tell him that everything is set up and you have rented a place for you both. He in turn will think that his plan has worked and if I am correct he will start the ball rolling before his release. I would think that he will go straight to the bank on his release and leave the country on the next available flight, with Melissa in tow, ready to cash in and start their new life of luxury abroad. However, we have seized his account and any money that is transferred into it will be held and returned to the bank when his crime is proven. Nathan will then receive a visit from the serious fraud squad and will spend considerably longer in prison as a result. Now all we need is to execute our plan. Right any questions?" There is silence as we all take it in. I realise that for the other four this is all common place but for Joseph and myself it is like something out of a film plot. Looking over at him I can see that he is deep in thought. Looking up he says, "Does Vanessa know any of this?" Shaking her head their boss says, "No, we can't risk word getting out and everyone panicking as a result. One banking crisis is more than enough. I am confident that we can contain everything and get the desired result." Looking once more around the table she says, "If there are no more questions we will call it a night. Melissa and Joseph we will need you tomorrow, Ben you must take Bella home but then return here as we could do with your help in tying this all up." Turning to me she says, "Thank you for your help with this Bella. Once again you have been dragged in to a situation which was not of your making. Let's just hope that this is the last time that you are." Before I can even reply she sweeps out of the room closely followed by Pete. Melissa laughs saying, "Good old Zo, you could never accuse her of letting the grass grow under her feet for a minute. What would we do without her?" With interest I say, "Is that her name, Zoe?" Melissa looks incredulous and says, "What all this time and you don't even know her name?" I nod and Joseph also looks interested. Grinning at Ben Melissa says, "Well that is something you will have to ask her about, it's not worth me getting in trouble for, hey Ben." Looking embarrassed Ben just says, "Come on Bella, it's going to be a long night, I'll take you home." We leave but I vow to ask him on the way, I mean what's in a name?

Chapter 44

On the way home I say, "Ben, what is your boss's name and why is it such a secret?" Ben smiles saying, "I knew that you would ask after Melissa's sidestepping. It's no great mystery really just something that we take for granted now." Confused I say, "What on earth does that mean?" Laughing he says, "In our organisation we tend to use codenames when we are working. Her real name is never used and we just call her by her codename. To outsiders it would seem strange but for us it is normal and we don't think much about it. However we don't use it amongst outsiders to avoid any awkward questions." Now I am even more confused and feeling annoyed say, "Oh for goodness sake just tell me her name!" Once again Ben laughs and says, "It's Zodiac, or Zo for short." Feeling surprised I think about it and say, "So what's your code name?" Smiling wickedly at me Ben says, "Aries." Snorting I say, "Well that figures. Trust you to be the ram. Let me guess, everyone's names a star sign?" He nods and I remember once hearing them refer to someone as Scorpio. Things begin to fall into place and I say, "What about Melissa?" He smiles saying, "Gemini." Thoughtfully I say, "Does this mean that there are only places for thirteen of you in your organisation?" Ben nods. "There are only twelve operatives with Zodiac in charge. When one leaves another takes their place. We are all chosen to balance each other, just like the signs of the Zodiac. Each one of us fulfils a certain role. It is the name of our organisation. Operation Zodiac. It is a top secret organisation and I am only telling you because you know so much about it already and have by default become an honorary member." I sit here digesting the information. "So is Pete considered an operative too and if he is what's his codename?" Ben looks at me, a slight smile on his face. "Pete is Capricorn. He no longer works in the field but acts as a link between Zo and the rest of us. He is her next in command and does all of the organising and planning." My mind is working away and I say, "Is that what you will do from now on? I mean will you be able to be part of the team and not work in the field?" Nodding he says, "Oh yes, there are many jobs that make up the organisation. Every one of them is vital for the success of the operation and my role will be to support those in the field. It's the best of both worlds. I get to have a normal life as well as work in an interesting and stimulating job doing what I love." I sit silently for a few minutes and then ask, "Does Pete have a family?" Ben goes quiet and I wonder if he heard me, but then he says, "Not as such, but he does have a partner." Feeling curious I say, "What's her name, does she work there too or is she like me, just an observer?" Grinning at me Ben says, "Her name is Bethany, and yes she does work for the organisation. Now question time over, we're here now and I have to drop you off and go straight back." Feeling disappointed I say, "Can't you even come in for a bit?" Ben grins wickedly saying, "As much as I'd like to come in, for a bit, I have work to do. Just make sure that you have a rest and remember don't breathe a word of what you have heard today to anyone." Leaning over to kiss him I say, "Your secret's safe with me - Aries."

I don't hear from Ben for the whole of the next day and despite being curious I remember that there are no phones allowed in their offices and realise that he is probably still working. I can't concentrate on much though as all I can think about is what is happening in London. I don't even want to speak to anyone as I am so jumpy I don't want to raise their suspicions that anything is up. Instead I decide to spring clean the house.
A few hours later and I feel well and truly exhausted. I have left no stone left unturned and it had the desired effect of distracting me from events in London. As I make myself a coffee I am surprised to hear a knock at the front door. I am even more surprised though when I answer it and see Joseph standing there. "Joseph, what a

pleasant surprise. Come in." I say, opening the door for him to follow me. He looks a bit guilty and says, "Thanks Bella. I'm sorry to disturb you but Ben thought it may do us good to have a chat, well me at any rate." Looking at him in surprise I say, "Ben said that?" He laughs saying, "I know, it surprised me too. I think that he realised that I needed to talk to somebody about all of this and I had nobody else to talk to who knew about it." As I make us a drink I say, "What happened this morning?" Joseph raises his eyes and sits down heavily on the settee. "Well Melissa and I went to the prison as arranged. I told my brother that you had been arrested and it was likely that Nathan would be released." "What did he say to that?" Looking annoyed Joseph says, "Oh he couldn't care less. All he wanted to know was if I had the money that Nathan had promised us for delivering Melissa." Carrying on he says, "Melissa played her part and we returned to the office. Whilst we were there we noticed that Nathan used his mobile to set up a transaction from the bank to his account. There wasn't enough to ring any alarm bells but he has obviously started his plan. We also watched as his solicitor visited him in prison and gave him the good news. Now Nathan believes that first thing tomorrow morning he will be out of there, a free man. Pete reckons that he will step up his plan with the bank over night and by the time he is released and on a plane somewhere the money would have been transferred and he would be away Scot free before they traced it to him." Sitting opposite him I let out a deep breath. "I would like to see his reaction when he hears that it has all been for nothing." Joseph laughs saying, "I think that he is due a visit from the fraud squad in the morning, rather than a goodbye from his fellow inmates. With any luck the bank won't be disrupted and nobody will be any the wiser." Nodding in agreement I look at him thoughtfully. "What about you Joseph. This visit wasn't just to update me was it?" Smiling Joseph says, "No, I just wanted to talk something through with you." He suddenly looks a bit anxious and I know what is coming. "You've been offered a new job haven't you and you're wondering about taking it." Smiling he says, "Is it that obvious?" Laughing I say, "Well it's no surprise to me. You're a natural for the role. You have already proved that you can keep up with the best of them and your computer skills, not to say anything about your other, shall we say more social skills, they would be hard pressed to find a better candidate. You also fit the brief of someone with no ties and able to devote yourself to the job 24 hours. What are you concerned about?" Grinning he says, "Well if you put it like that I suppose there's nothing standing in my way. I just feel a bit out of my depth

that's all. I know they will provide training but it's a huge move from escort to spy don't you think?"
Nodding in agreement I say, "Yes it is, however it is one transition that I think you could make easily. They look after their own and you would certainly have an exciting life. You could use it to set yourself up for life and who knows it may lead on to other things."
I can feel Joseph's eyes burning into me as he speaks. "I always wanted what you and Ben have. My childhood wasn't a great one and I used to look with envy at my friends and their loving families. I crave that life for myself. I want to meet someone, settle down and have a family one day. This job is not without its dangers, Melissa is proof of that. I'm not saying that the thought of it doesn't excite me but what if I make the wrong choice?"
Moving over I sit down next to him and to his surprise take his hand in mine. Squeezing it I look into his eyes and say sincerely, "You will find everything that you want Joseph. The trouble is you can't rush it, it will happen when you least expect it. In the meantime you should take advantage of this amazing offer. It will give you a purpose and open up a huge amount of doors to you. You will be your own man, not just an accessory for a rich client. It may only last a short time before like Ben you find where you really want to be, but even Ben

can't turn his back on it completely. He loves the organisation, it's in his blood. It's your choice but don't chase the what ifs and maybes deal with the here and now and the rest will follow."
Looking grateful Joseph says, "I agree with you 100% Bella. I just needed to hear somebody else say it. You've been a good friend to me and I hope that our friendship will continue for many more years." Smiling gently at him I say, "I'll always be here for you Joseph and so will Ben. You're family now and don't you forget it."

Chapter 45

3 weeks later

Waiting for my next Rep to call I think back over the last few weeks. As expected everything fell into place and Nathan was once again arrested, whilst still in prison, for framing Ben and I and stealing from the stores and the bank. By all accounts he didn't take the news well and had to be restrained by four prison officers when he found out. Joseph started his new job and Ben tells me that he is doing extremely well in the training. Ben is now home again for good this time and we cannot be any happier than we are. We had some explaining to do though and managed to smooth everything over with my family and Phoebe and Boris with just a few white lies. I hope that I will never ever have to go through anything like it again and all I want now is a quiet life.

I am interrupted by April moaning as she hits her computer in frustration. "I hate this new system. I don't know what on earth was wrong with the old one. Why do they do these things just to annoy me?" Laughing at her I don't tell her the real reason for the change. Obviously we couldn't take any chances and replaced the whole computer system in all of the stores. I know that the bank did too so hopefully there will be no more repeats of the problems that we had. There is also a new store manager due to start next week and I just hope that he is middle aged and as ugly as anything. I am interrupted by a call from the shop floor. Apparently my next appointment is here so I head off to meet them. However I am surprised to find that it's not the rep that I was expecting. Turning to face me, looking amazing is Vanessa. Smiling shyly at me she says, "Hello Bella. I hope that you don't mind me turning up like this." Feeling shocked I just look at her in amazement. Gathering myself I say, "No, not at all. It's good to see you again." Looking nervous she says, "I was hoping for a chance to have a chat with you, possibly over a coffee? There's something that I need to say and it's long overdue." Feeling worried I look at my watch saying, "I would love to Vanessa. I am expecting a rep any minute now so let me just ask my assistant to see them for me. Can you just give me a minute?" Smiling she says, "Of course. I'll wait here until you are ready."

It doesn't take me long and I am soon back with her. "Let's go to the coffee shop and I'll get you that coffee." I say, wondering what on earth she wants to talk about. As she follows me she says, "Let me buy the drinks Bella, it's the least I can do after the trouble I caused you." It doesn't take us long and we are soon sitting opposite each other with our coffees. Looking at her expectantly, I wonder what she has come to say. Nervously she clears her throat and then speaks in a quiet voice. "I owe you an apology for causing you so much trouble over the last few months." Ignoring my attempts to reassure her she says, "The trouble is as soon as I thought Ben was in trouble it made me determined to save him. Joseph told me what his brother had said and I am afraid I believed every word." Looking wistful she says, "Joseph has also been a good friend to me and told me because he was worried about me. He knew that I was an investor in the stores and didn't want to see me lose my investment. He also believed his brother, I mean why wouldn't we?" Taking a sip of her coffee I can tell that she is nervous. "Look Vanessa, it doesn't matter. You did what you thought was best for you and for Ben. It's in the past now and we must all forget about it and move on." Looking nervously at me she says, "I know but I also owe you an explanation about my relationship with Ben. He means everything to me, but not in the way you think." Suddenly I feel excited. I can tell that she is going to tell me something about their past and I wonder if I'm ready to hear it.

Clearing her throat Vanessa looks nervously at me. "I know that Ben has told you something of my past. I was married to a truly repulsive individual who made me sink as low as a person can get. I never knew the true meaning of love until Ben came into my life." Her eyes soften and she looks wistful. Feeling uncomfortable I wait to hear what she says next. "I fell in love with Ben more than I had ever loved anyone before and never have since." Sensing how I must be feeling she smiles reassuringly. "It's ok Bella, nothing to worry about. Ben saved me at a time when I was at my lowest point. He taught me that life was worth living and showed me the true meaning of love. My husband seeing that I had changed began to show more of an interest in me. I was having an affair with Ben at the time and he could see that I was a changed woman. He wanted what he could no longer have and when he couldn't get it willingly he took it unwillingly." I feel sick hearing what she has to say. I almost can't look at her such is the hurt in her face and I wonder why she is telling me all of this. Shaking as if to dispel the unhappy memories she says sadly. "I realised that I had to do something and soon. The night he raped and beat me I made a vow to myself. It would be the last time. Ben asked me to go away with him. He was appalled at what he found when he came to the house. I couldn't just leave though. Claude was my husband and the Chairman of my family business. I had too much to lose so I began to think of a way that I could get him out of my life completely. That is where Ben

helped me. I will be forever grateful to him because he delved as deep as anybody could and uncovered the true extent of my husbands philandering ways. There was quite a dossier on him both in his business life and his personal one. He had quite the chequered history and was running my families business into the ground. Ben collated all of the evidence, enough for me to destroy Claude. I wanted him out of my life for good with nothing to show for it than what he could carry."
Hearing her speak in her softly spoken voice I am mesmerised. It is like something out of a film plot and I hold onto her every word. Looking directly at me she says, "The evening that Claude died I had everything planned. I waited until he had returned home from seeing his latest mistress. When he came back I confronted him. His bags were packed and waiting for him by the door. I told him that I was divorcing him on the grounds of his adultery and that he would be sacked from his position at the bank for gross misconduct." Her voice falters and it is as if she is reliving it in front of me. "He just laughed and moved towards me threateningly. He was a vile man and I tried to stand my ground but he was a bully. I found myself backing into his study and I quickly placed myself so that the desk was between us. He told me that I could never divorce him. No court in the land would believe me over him

and he would have me admitted to the mental institution quicker than I could blink. I told him that I was stronger now and had documented proof of his wrong doings but he just laughed, an evil laugh." I notice that Vanessa's eyes fill with tears and she says in a whisper. "I watched as he removed his belt from his trousers. He wrapped the leather around his hands until the buckle end was dangling in front of him. He started towards me saying that it was time he taught me a lesson once and for all. He said that he was going to enjoy the experience and when he had finished beating me with his belt he was going to punish me by showing me who was boss. I knew what that meant. The last time he had showed me who was boss his attack lasted long into the night. I knew that he was much stronger than me and if I was going to get away I didn't have much time." She breaks off and puts her head in her hands. I can tell that she is once again back in that study and my heart goes out to her. I reach over the table and take her hand in mine and smile reassuringly at her. "It's ok Vanessa, you're safe now." Straightening up she looks fearfully at me and says, "I did the only thing I knew. Quickly I reached into the top drawer of the desk. I knew that Claude had a gun in there and I swear I just wanted to warn him off. He saw where I was heading and raced over to stop me. It was so confusing and before I knew what was happening the gun went off. It didn't register at first but then I saw him. He had fallen onto the desk head first. I knew at once he was dead, I had killed him." Tears run down her face and her voice is almost a whisper. "I didn't know what to do so I did the first thing that came to my mind. I called Ben. He came quickly and I broke down. I must have gone into shock because I don't remember what happened next. The next thing I knew I woke up in bed the next day and when I went downstairs the house was full of police and scenes of crime officers. Ben saw me coming down the stairs and together with a police officer they sat me down and told me that Claude had committed suicide and I had found him and gone into a state of shock. The doctor had prescribed a sedative and now that I was awake they needed to ask me some questions. As they carried on with them I realised that Ben must have covered up my involvement and called the police. Apparently the bullet had entered the side of his head and they thought that it was self inflicted. Ben must have wiped my prints from the gun and placed it in Claude's hand." Looking at me with wide eyes Vanessa says, "So you see Ben saved me. Not only once but twice. I could never have survived without him and I owe him everything. He risked a great deal for me and I will forever be in his debt." Shaken I lean back my mind buzzing from her confession. Ben was an accomplice to murder. I know that it was an accident and self defence but even so. Leaning forward Vanessa says. "Don't think badly of him Bella. He did what he thought was best. I was in no state to go through a trial and the bank wouldn't survive another scandal. That is why I gave him the money for the stores. He needed a future and I wanted to give it to him as he had done for me. I am happy that he found you. We were lovers once but could never be again. Instead I am happier alone with no relationship ties. I use the services of people like Joseph and it is the way I want it to be. Ben and I were there for each other when we both needed it and will forever be together as friends. I am sorry to tell you this but I wanted you to know the full facts. There should be no secrets between you and I know that this particular one wasn't his to tell. Please don't think badly of either of us." As I look at her I just feel so much sadness for her. Despite the trappings of wealth life hadn't been kind to her. I understand why Ben did what he did, and I love him even more for it.

After a short while Vanessa stands up saying. "Thank you for hearing me out and not judging me Bella. I would like us to be friends too and I just hope that we can be after what I have done." I go over and hug her to her surprise. "Thank you Vanessa. It must have taken a lot for you to tell me what you just have. I don't think badly of you at all. If I had been in your position I would have probably done the same thing. You deserve to be happy now." Smiling and looking relieved Vanessa says farewell and I return to the store a changed person.

When Ben returns home from work he looks at me with worry on his face. I race over and hug him as tightly as I can. His body relaxes and I can tell that he was worried. Kissing the top of my head he says, "I know that Vanessa told you. She rang and said that she had." Pulling away I can see the stress in his face. "It's ok Ben. You did what you had to do. I would have probably done the same in your position." Raising his eyes up he grins at me. "Really, you think?" Pushing him in mock anger he catches my hands and draws me down beside him on to the settee. Looking hard at me he says, "Actually it's not what you think." Confused I say, "What isn't?" Leaning back he pulls me against him. "Vanessa thinks that I covered it all up to save her. That bit is true but I didn't do the covering up." Pulling away I look at him in surprise. "Then who did?"
Looking steadily at me he says, "It was Zodiac. When I got there Vanessa was in shock. She didn't register anything I said and so I called Pete. Zo and Pete came to the house and brought with them our doctor. He gave Vanessa a sedative and then we all set about making it

look as though Claude had committed suicide." I know that I must look shocked and say, "But why? Surely any court in the land would have found her not guilty, what with all the evidence you had gathered." Shaking his head Ben says, "You forget Bella, I was on an operation. The bank was under investigation and Claude was our man. We couldn't risk any scandal because the banking world was in crisis. Vanessa didn't know anything about our organisation and it was decided that this was to our advantage. Claude would be removed from the picture and we would repair the damage he had caused. Vanessa would be free of him and there would be no awkward questions. Sometimes the best laid plans go wrong, just look at Melissa. This was actually the best way forward and would save a lot of problems in the future. We did what we had to do for the sake of everyone involved. Sometimes that happens."

Part of me is glad that Ben hadn't done it and the other part of me wonders what else he has had to do for the sake of his operation. Shuddering I am glad that he is no longer at risk out there. Turning towards him I kiss him gently on the lips. Crushing me to him he kisses me back passionately and deeply. As I feel him close to me everything else ceases to matter. We made it through. No more secrets and just a lifetime to enjoy being together.

Epilogue

She smiled as Pete entered the room. Crossing over to her she tilted her head as he bent to kiss her. Pulling her up towards him he held her in his vice like grip. Running her fingers around the back of his head she pulled him closer and arched her body towards him. God she needed him so much, in every way possible. He was the blood in her veins and the air that she breathed. Without him she had nothing. Pulling back she smiled seductively up at him.
"Another job well done darling. Maybe we can take that holiday we have been promising ourselves." Arching his eyebrows he says, "I'll believe that when I see it." Knowing that he is probably right she sits down again back at her desk. Flicking a flirtatious look in his direction she says, "Later babes. Right now we still have work to do." Sighing heavily Pete sits down on the desk, adjacent to her. "What's next?" Thoughtfully she picks up her pen and chews the end. "A job has just come in that requires two operatives, a man and a woman. What do you think about pitting the old against the new?" Grinning wickedly at her he says, "I knew you wouldn't be able to wait to test out your new toy." Laughing she

says, "And such a fine one too. Let's see what he's made of shall we?"
Leaning over Pete turns off the lamp on her desk. Let's just leave Zodiac here for the night. I want to take my girl home." Pulling her up he picks her off her feet. "Come on Bethany, I've got plans for you."

The End

If you have enjoyed this book it would be very kind of you to leave me a review on Amazon I am always grateful for these and read every one.

Coming Soon

Operation Zodiac

Starting with Bethany's story

Don't miss out on the exciting new series. Sign up at my website for teasers and special offers.

sjcrabb.com

Newly Published

Falcondell

The Devil's Son

Grace Gray is sent to Falcondell High to finish High School with her cousin Gabe as her protector. She has moved around all of her life and longs for a normal life. Unfortunately for her she is far from normal and has to join the "Invisibles" in order to pass through the year unnoticed. Nobody must discover her secret.

The hottest, meanest, most evil bad boy that you could ever wish to meet in the school though has other ideas and is used to getting his own way. Ash Knight lives with his uncle who controls the Town through fear. He is the leader of the most feared gang in the area and nobody gets in their way. Ash lives with his uncle but spends his holidays with his father.

When Grace comes to Falcondell Ash finds himself in unknown territory. They say that opposites attract but this relationship is the stuff of nightmares for everyone involved. They will have to not only battle their own feelings but those of their families and friends. Will Grace's guardians allow them to be together or will she once again be moved away for her own protection? Ash also discovers something that turns his world upside down and they both end up fighting for a lot more than each other.

If you like a good High school romance with a bad boy to die for then this is for you.

Can somebody who is so good ever be with somebody

who is completely evil? Ash and Grace are at opposite sides of the spectrum and this year changes them both forever.

Printed in Great Britain
by Amazon